NTSB/RAR-12/02
PB2012-916302
Notation 8400
Adopted April 24, 2012

Railroad Accident Report

Collision of BNSF Coal Train With the Rear End of Standing
BNSF Maintenance-of-Way Equipment Train
Red Oak, Iowa
April 17, 2011

**National
Transportation
Safety Board**

490 L'Enfant Plaza, S.W.
Washington, D.C. 20594

National Transportation Safety Board. 2012. *Collision of BNSF Coal Train With the Rear End of Standing BNSF Maintenance-of-Way Equipment Train, Red Oak, Iowa, April 17, 2011.* **Railroad Accident Report NTSB/RAR-12/02. Washington, D.C.**

Abstract: On April 17, 2011, about 6:55 a.m. central daylight time, eastbound BNSF Railway coal train C-BTMCNM0-26, BNSF 9159 East, travelling about 23 mph, collided with the rear end of standing BNSF Railway maintenance-of-way equipment train U-BRGCRI-15, BNSF 9470 East, near Red Oak, Iowa. The accident occurred near milepost 448.3 on main track number two on the Creston Subdivision of the BNSF Railway Nebraska Division. The collision resulted in the derailment of 2 locomotives and 12 cars. As a result of collision forces, the lead locomotive's modular crew cab was detached, partially crushed, and involved in a subsequent diesel fuel fire. Both crewmembers on the striking train were fatally injured. Damage was in excess of $8.7 million.

The National Transportation Safety Board is an independent Federal agency dedicated to promoting aviation, railroad, highway, marine, pipeline, and hazardous materials safety. Established in 1967, the agency is mandated by Congress through the Independent Safety Board Act of 1974 to investigate transportation accidents, determine the probable causes of the accidents, issue safety recommendations, study transportation safety issues, and evaluate the safety effectiveness of government agencies involved in transportation. The Safety Board makes public its actions and decisions through accident reports, safety studies, special investigation reports, safety recommendations, and statistical reviews.

Recent publications are available in their entirety on the Internet at <http://www.ntsb.gov>. Other information about available publications also may be obtained from the website or by contacting:

National Transportation Safety Board
Records Management Division, CIO-40
490 L'Enfant Plaza, SW
Washington, D.C. 20594
(800) 877-6799 or (202) 314-6551

Safety Board publications may be purchased, by individual copy or by subscription, from the National Technical Information Service. To purchase this publication, order report number PB2012-916302 from:

National Technical Information Service
5285 Port Royal Road
Springfield, Virginia 22161
(800) 553-6847 or (703) 605-6000

The Independent Safety Board Act, as codified at 49 U.S.C. Section 1154(b), precludes the admission into evidence or use of Board reports related to an incident or accident in a civil action for damages resulting from a matter mentioned in the report.

Contents

Figures

Acronyms and Abbreviations

AAR	Association of American Railroads
Amtrak	National Railroad Passenger Corporation
BMI	Body mass index
BNSF	BNSF Railway
CP	Control point
EMD	Electro-Motive Diesel, Inc.
ERP	Employee review process
ETMS	Electronic Train Management System
FIRE	Functionally Integrated Railroad Equipment
FRA	Federal Railroad Administration
GCOR	General Code of Operating Rules
IC	Incident commander
MOW	Maintenance of way
MP	Milepost
NOC	Network operations center
NPRM	Notice of Proposed Rulemaking
NTSB	National Transportation Safety Board
psi	Pounds per square inch
PTC	Positive train control
ROFD	Red Oak Fire Department
RSAC	Rail Safety Advisory Committee
RSIA	Railroad Safety Improvement Act
TPOB	Tons per operative brake
UP	Union Pacific Railroad

Executive Summary

On April 17, 2011, about 6:55 a.m. central daylight time, eastbound BNSF Railway coal train C-BTMCNM0-26, BNSF 9159 East, travelling about 23 mph, collided with the rear end of standing BNSF Railway maintenance-of-way equipment train U-BRGCRI-15, BNSF 9470 East, near Red Oak, Iowa. The accident occurred near milepost 448.3 on main track number two on the Creston Subdivision of the BNSF Railway Nebraska Division. The collision resulted in the derailment of 2 locomotives and 12 cars. As a result of collision forces, the lead locomotive's modular crew cab was detached, partially crushed, and involved in a subsequent diesel fuel fire. Both crewmembers on the striking train were fatally injured. Damage was in excess of $8.7 million.

The National Transportation Safety Board determines that the probable cause of the accident was the failure of the crew of the striking train to comply with the signal indication requiring them to operate in accordance with restricted speed requirements and stop short of the standing train because they had fallen asleep due to fatigue resulting from their irregular work schedules and their medical conditions. Contributing to the accident was the absence of a positive train control system that identifies the rear of a train and stops a following train if a safe braking profile is exceeded. Contributing to the severity of collision damage to the locomotive cab of the striking coal train was the absence of crashworthiness standards for modular locomotive crew cabs.

The safety issues identified during this accident investigation are as follows:

- Train crew fatigue

- Positive train control regulations and design

- Crashworthiness of modular locomotive cabs

- Survivability of electronic data

As a result of this accident investigation, the National Transportation Safety Board makes safety recommendations to the Federal Railroad Administration, the Association of American Railroads, and the BNSF Railway. The National Transportation Safety Board also reiterates recommendations previously issued to the Federal Railroad Administration.

1. Factual Information

1.1 Accident Synopsis

On April 17, 2011, about 6:55[1] a.m. central daylight time, eastbound BNSF Railway[2] (BNSF) coal train C-BTMCNM0-26, BNSF 9159 East, collided with the rear end of standing BNSF maintenance-of-way (MOW) equipment train U-BRGCRI-15, BNSF 9470 East, near Red Oak, Iowa. (See figure 1.) The accident occurred on a curve near milepost (MP) 448.3 on main track number two (track two) on the Creston Subdivision of the BNSF Nebraska Division. The striking coal train was travelling about 23 mph when it struck the standing MOW equipment train.

Figure 1. Accident location.

As a result of the collision, the two lead locomotives of the striking train derailed along with the first two coal cars. The modular crew cab on the lead locomotive of the striking train was detached, partially crushed, and involved in a subsequent diesel fuel fire. Seven additional coal cars were also damaged but did not derail. The 10 rear cars of the struck train derailed. Both the engineer and the conductor on the striking train were fatally injured in the collision. The crew on the locomotive of the struck train reported non-life-threatening injuries. Damages were estimated at more than $8.7 million. The

---

[1] All times in this report are central daylight time.

[2] The BNSF Railway was created on September 22, 1995, from the merger of Burlington Northern Inc. (parent company of Burlington Northern Railroad) and Santa Fe Pacific Corporation (parent company of the Atchison, Topeka and Santa Fe Railway). On February 12, 2010, the BNSF became a subsidiary of Berkshire Hathaway, Inc.

weather at the time of the accident was reported as 5 miles' visibility, with mist at Red Oak airport, which is about 3 1/2 miles east of the accident location.

Event recorder data from the lead locomotive of the striking train indicate that before the collision, train speed increased and the throttle was decreased as the train crested a hill west of the accident site. The last throttle reduction occurred 1 minute 53 seconds before impact. The train's brakes were not applied before impact.

1.2   Preaccident Events

1.2.1   MOW Equipment Train (Struck Train)

The engineer and the conductor of the struck MOW equipment train went on duty in Lincoln, Nebraska, at 1:15 a.m., and their train departed about 3:15 a.m. Investigators interviewed the crew and were told that up until the collision, the trip was unremarkable.

At railroad control point[3] (CP) 4580, the MOW equipment train entered track two behind two eastbound coal trains, neither of which was involved in this collision. The MOW equipment train stopped at a red stop signal[4] at CP 4535 (MP 453.5) because two coal trains were ahead on track two and the first had stopped at the end of the multiple tracks at CP McPherson (MP 447.5). (The milepost numbers were decreasing in an eastward direction). (See figure 2.)

---

[3] A *control point* is a location on the railroad where the train dispatcher can control train movements by setting routes. CP 4580 is a point where a single track diverges eastward into two main tracks.

[4] See appendix B for illustrations and explanations of signal aspects and indications.

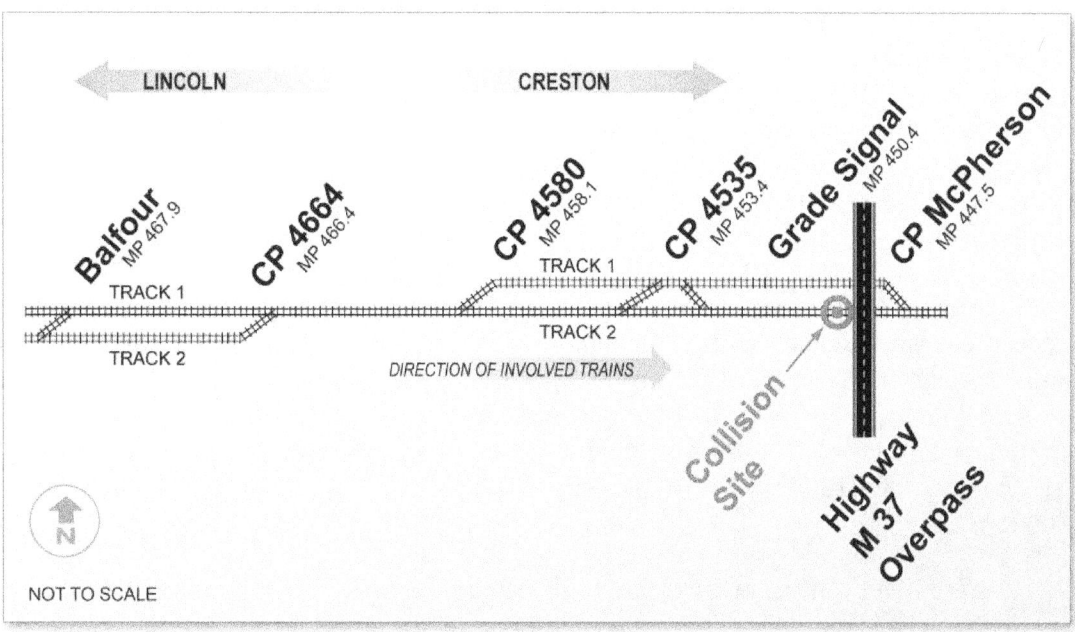

Figure 2. Track map of accident area.

The first uninvolved coal train received a proceed signal and entered the single track east of CP McPherson. The second uninvolved coal train then moved eastward on track two and stopped at CP McPherson. The MOW equipment train followed, having received a yellow approach signal at CP 4535. The MOW equipment train then encountered a red (restricting) "grade signal"[5] at MP 450.38 and continued at restricted speed[6] until stopping about 300 feet behind the second uninvolved coal train.

While these two trains were stopped at the east end of the multiple tracks on track two, Amtrak (National Railroad Passenger Corporation) No. 6 (the California Zephyr) passed them going eastward on main track number one (track one) about 6:22 a.m.

The second uninvolved coal train then received a signal to proceed east and followed Amtrak No. 6. The MOW equipment train then moved up to CP McPherson and stopped at the red stop signal.

1.2.2 Striking Coal Train

The engineer and the conductor of the striking coal train went on duty in Lincoln, Nebraska, at 2:31 a.m. After completing the required airbrake test, their train departed about 3:45 a.m.

---

[5] A *grade signal* is used on an incline (grade) where it may be difficult to restart a stopped train, and it permits trains to pass a red aspect without stopping but requires further movement to be at restricted speed.

[6] *Restricted speed* on the BNSF requires operating prepared to stop short of a train ahead within one-half the range of vision, not to exceed 20 mph.

While the two uninvolved coal trains and the MOW equipment train were on track two between CP 4580 and CP McPherson, the striking coal train was stopped at Balfour (MP 467.9) on track two. About 6:08 a.m., Amtrak No. 6 passed the striking coal train on the adjacent track, and the Amtrak engineer told NTSB investigators that he was able to see the crewmember on the conductor's side of the striking coal train's lead locomotive. He reported that the crewmember he had observed was in a reclining position.[7]

After it was passed by Amtrak No. 6, the striking coal train received a signal to proceed eastward. It moved onto the single main track at CP 4664 and then entered the multiple main tracks at CP 4580 on track two. Maximum authorized track speed at the accident location was 79 mph for passenger trains and 60 mph for freight trains. The striking coal train was further restricted to 45 mph because its tons per operative brake (TPOB) exceeded 100 (actual TPOB was 142.5). Signal indications can further restrict train speeds.

Based on event recorder data and dispatcher records, the striking coal train's trip was without incident before it reached the crest of the grade about 2 miles before the collision. Figure 3 shows 6 miles of the track profile in the area of the collision and includes the positions of the signals, the peak of the grade, and the two trains involved in this accident about 15 minutes before the collision.

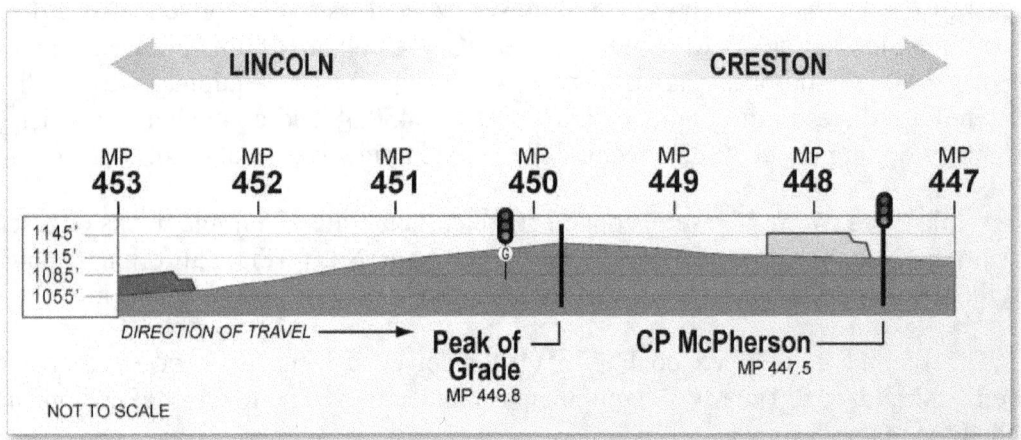

Figure 3. Track profile between MP 453 and MP 447.

---

[7] BNSF operating rules permit one crewmember to nap while stopped waiting to be met or passed by another train.

Signal system recorder data indicated that the striking coal train passed a yellow approach signal at CP 4535 and then the red "restricting" grade signal at MP 450.38 that protected the rear end of the standing MOW equipment train. Locomotive event recorder data indicated that the striking coal train had passed CP 4535 while moving about 30 mph in throttle position 1. The striking coal train's speed reduced to about 12 mph, and its throttle was in position 7 when the train passed the red restricting grade signal at MP 450.38 approaching the top of the 0.6-percent grade. The speed reduction was consistent with the signal indication, grade, tonnage, and the amount of power the engineer had applied. Until reaching MP 449.4 the striking coal train engineer maintained the speed at between 11 and 12 mph using throttle adjustments. As the striking coal train crested the grade, train speed increased from 11 mph to 23 mph at the point of collision. There were several throttle adjustments during the last 15 minutes of the trip as shown in figure 4, but no activity was detected during the last 1 minute 53 seconds. At impact, the throttle was in throttle position 4, and brakes had not been applied.

Figure 4 was developed from event recorder data from the striking train's lead locomotive and shows when the engineer manipulated the controls of the locomotive between CP 4535 and the point of collision. The event recorder data is shown in tabular form at appendix C.

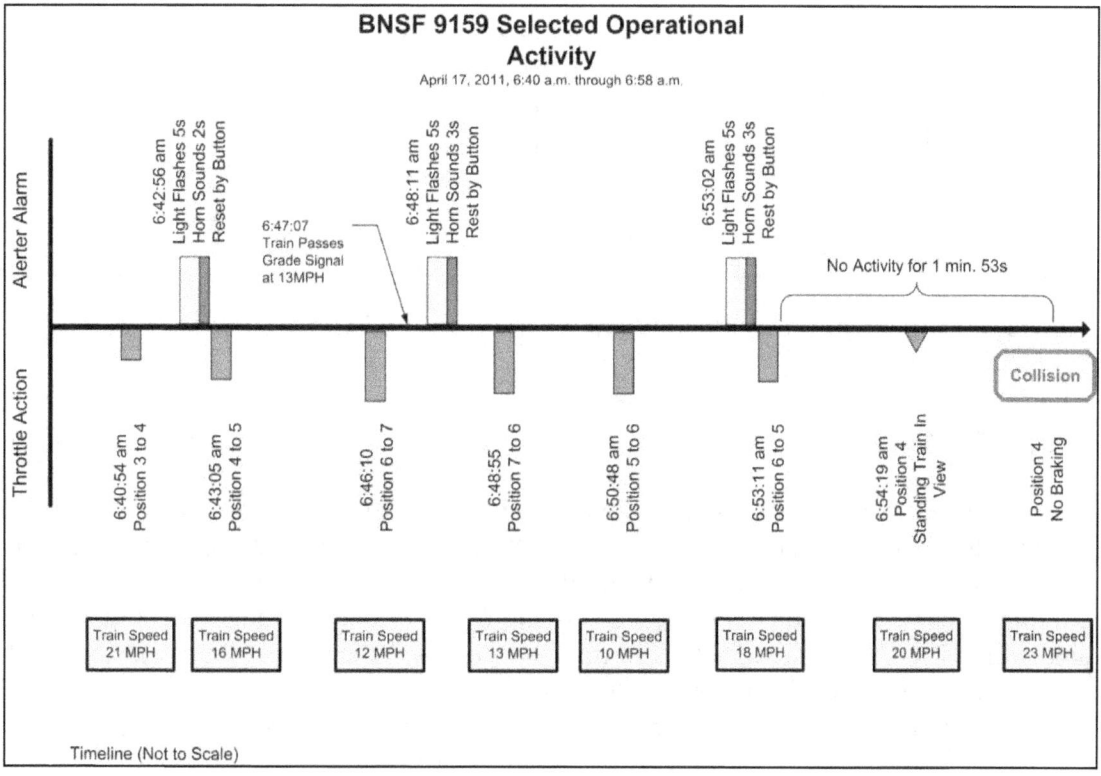

Figure 4. Event recorder data from locomotive of striking train.

Data from the striking train's (BNSF 9159) event recorder show that during the 15 minutes prior to the collision, the striking train's lead locomotive alerter alarmed three times after periods of engineer inactivity and was reset using the alerter reset button after a strobe displayed for 5 seconds and an audible alarm sounded for an additional 2 to 3 seconds. The collision occurred 1 minute 53 seconds after a throttle movement, and the alerter would have been due to alarm in about 7 seconds had the collision not occurred. Figure 5 shows the alerter alarm events that occurred during the last 15 minutes before the collision.

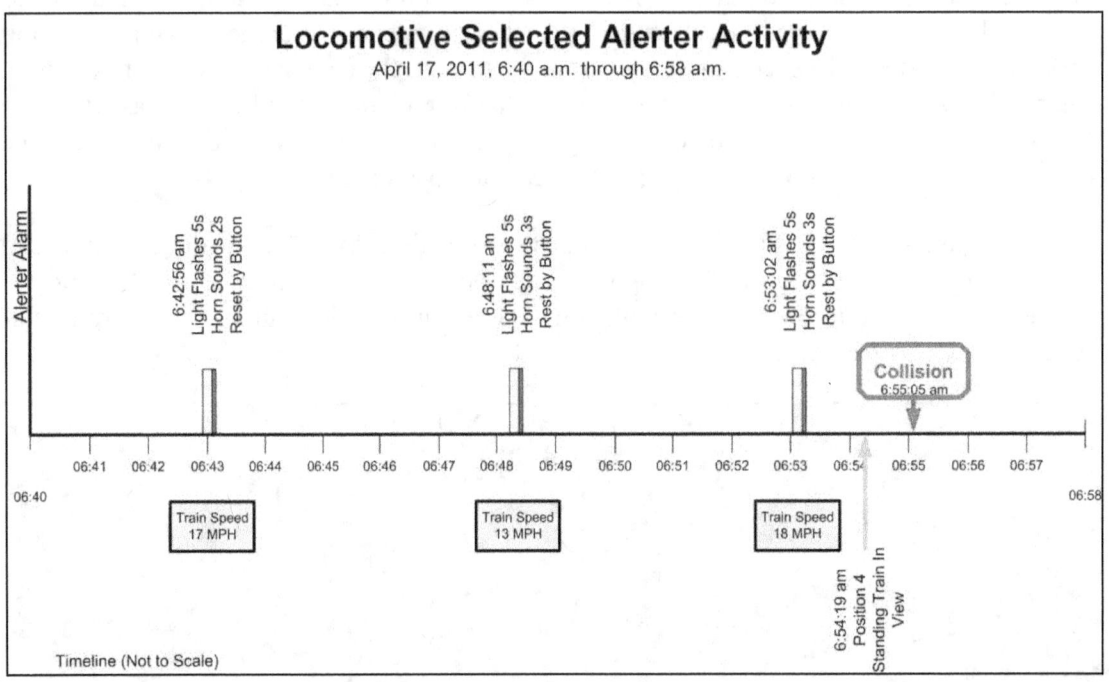

Figure 5. Alerter alarm events from striking train locomotive event recorder during last 15 minutes before collision.

1.2.3 The Collision

The striking coal train collided with the rear car of the standing MOW equipment train about MP 448.3. The rear car of the MOW equipment train was almost immediately crushed, derailed, and displaced to the north of the track. Several other pieces of derailed equipment came to rest on track one. (See figure 6.) At the same time as the collision, the signal circuit on track one registered a track occupancy indication at the BNSF Network Operations Center (NOC) in Fort Worth, Texas. Based on locomotive event recorder and signal system recorder data, the time of the collision was a few seconds after 6:55 a.m.

Figure 6. Wreckage including lead locomotive of striking train.

The striking train continued about 690 feet after the initial impact. The locomotive event recorder data indicated that following impact, the train speed dropped from 23 mph to 21 mph, and then the emergency brakes applied because of collision damage. The event recorder data indicated that neither the engineer nor the conductor activated the brakes before or after impact.

The crew on the MOW equipment train told investigators that while waiting at CP McPherson, they felt a strong impact that shoved their train forward; locomotive event recorder data from the MOW equipment train showed a movement of about 17 feet. The engineer said he knew that they had been rear-ended by another train. When he observed the rear of his train, he said, he saw a large smoke plume and fire, and he called 911. He left the cab and went toward the rear of the train. When he neared the rear of his train, he saw that the lead locomotive of the striking coal train (BNSF 9159) was on fire.

1.2.4 Injuries

Both crewmembers on the striking coal train were fatally injured. The engineer and the conductor on the MOW equipment train reported back and neck pain and sought medical treatment. No emergency responders were injured.

1.2.5 Damage

Total damage was estimated at more than $8.7 million and is detailed in table 1.

Table 1. Estimated damage.

Equipment and Other Costs	Estimated Damage
Coal train	$1,157,482
MOW train	195,411
MOW equipment on flatcars	5,140,000
Track	898,593
Wreckage removal and cleanup	875,386
Miscellaneous labor costs	79,288
Highway overpass	380,000
Total	**$8,726,151**

1.2.6 Wreckage

Struck Train. The last car (the 34th car behind the locomotive) on the MOW equipment train, Herzog clip car[8] HZGX-150, was the first car struck by locomotive BNSF 9159. The clip car was derailed and displaced near the point of collision to the north side of track two and caught fire. The clip car was folded roughly in half by collision forces. The powered wheel set from the clip car lodged at the base of the snow plow of the striking locomotive and was carried to the point of rest.

The next to the last car in the MOW equipment train was BNSF 927022 (the 33rd car), an 89-foot-long flatcar equipped with a Kershaw "Scorpion Ramp," which is a ramp that unfolds so that MOW equipment can roll on and off a flatcar, called a scorpion car. The struck end of this scorpion car overrode and came to rest on top of BNSF 9159 with the scorpion ramp extended across the top of the locomotive. The scorpion car was partially bent lengthwise, top toward the bottom, 20 feet from the "A" end[9] of the car. One truck assembly from this car came to rest on top of the short hood[10] assembly of BNSF 9159, toward the left side of the locomotive. The other truck assembly, along with a wheel set, came to rest in front of BNSF 9159.

---

[8] A *clip car* is maintenance-of-way equipment that installs clips that secure the rails to the tie plates on the ties.

[9] Each end of a freight car is designated as either the A or the B end. The hand brake is typically located on the B end.

[10] The locomotive *short hood* is a structure at the leading end of the cab containing the collision posts and the forward access door. It is further defined in the Association of American Railroads Manual of Standards and Recommended Practices, Standard S-580, revision 2005, "Locomotive Crashworthiness Requirements," which is a standard incorporated by reference in Title 49 *Code of Federal Regulations* 229.205.

The next four cars (the 29th through the 32nd cars behind the locomotive) were 89-foot-long flatcars loaded with MOW equipment that were derailed and displaced to the north side of track two near the Highway M 37 overpass. (See map in figure 2 and figures 7 and 8.) Much of the cargo on these cars (MOW equipment) broke free from securements and was scattered along the right-of-way.

Red Oak Fire Department photo

Figure 7. View of wreckage from highway overpass facing east.

Red Oak Fire Department photo

Figure 8. View of wreckage from highway overpass facing west.

The next three cars (26th through 28th) also were 89-foot-long flatcars that were loaded with MOW equipment. These cars, along with the scorpion flatcar, came to rest lying against each other and overriding each other and leaning against the front end of the lead locomotive of the striking train. (See figure 9.) Trucks, wheel sets, and MOW equipment were scattered along the north and south sides of the tracks.

Positioned in front of the snow plow of the lead locomotive of the striking train, BNSF 9159, from east to west, were the following:

- One powered wheel set from the clip car

- One truck frame from the clip car

- One wheel set from the clip car

- One truck assembly from BNSF flatcar 927022 (the 33rd car)

The last car to derail (25th) on the MOW equipment train was also an 89-foot-long flatcar loaded with MOW equipment. It derailed upright and generally in line with the track.

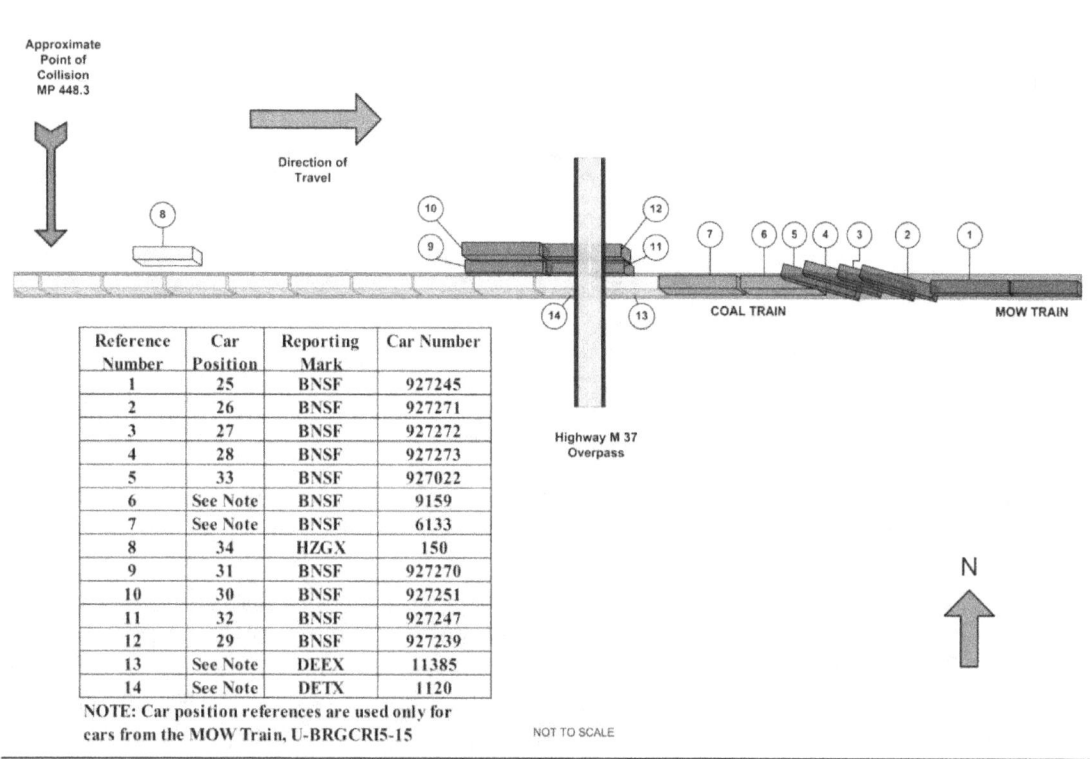

Reference Number	Car Position	Reporting Mark	Car Number
1	25	BNSF	927245
2	26	BNSF	927271
3	27	BNSF	927272
4	28	BNSF	927273
5	33	BNSF	927022
6	See Note	BNSF	9159
7	See Note	BNSF	6133
8	34	HZGX	150
9	31	BNSF	927270
10	30	BNSF	927251
11	32	BNSF	927247
12	29	BNSF	927239
13	See Note	DEEX	11385
14	See Note	DETX	1120

NOTE: Car position references are used only for cars from the MOW Train, U-BRGCRI5-15

NOT TO SCALE

Figure 9. Wreckage diagram (not to scale).

Striking Train. The lead locomotive of the striking coal train, BNSF 9159, sustained extensive frontal damage. (See figure 10.) It derailed, but the unit stayed upright and generally in line with the track. About 16 feet of the front end of BNSF 9159 was compromised as a result of the collision. The short hood and collision posts, normally positioned perpendicular to the deck, were pushed and deflected at an angle of about 35° to 40° in the direction of the cab. The end plate, snow plow, anti-climber,[11] short hood, and collision posts were severely damaged and deformed. A major impact area was identified on the front door frame of the operating cab. The frame was found to be split at the top right. The inner doorway, or vestibule, floor area had indications of severe loading and was bent rearward and upward.

---

[11] *Anti-climbers* are located at the ends of adjoining cars in a train and are designed to engage when subjected to large compressive (buff) loads to prevent override.

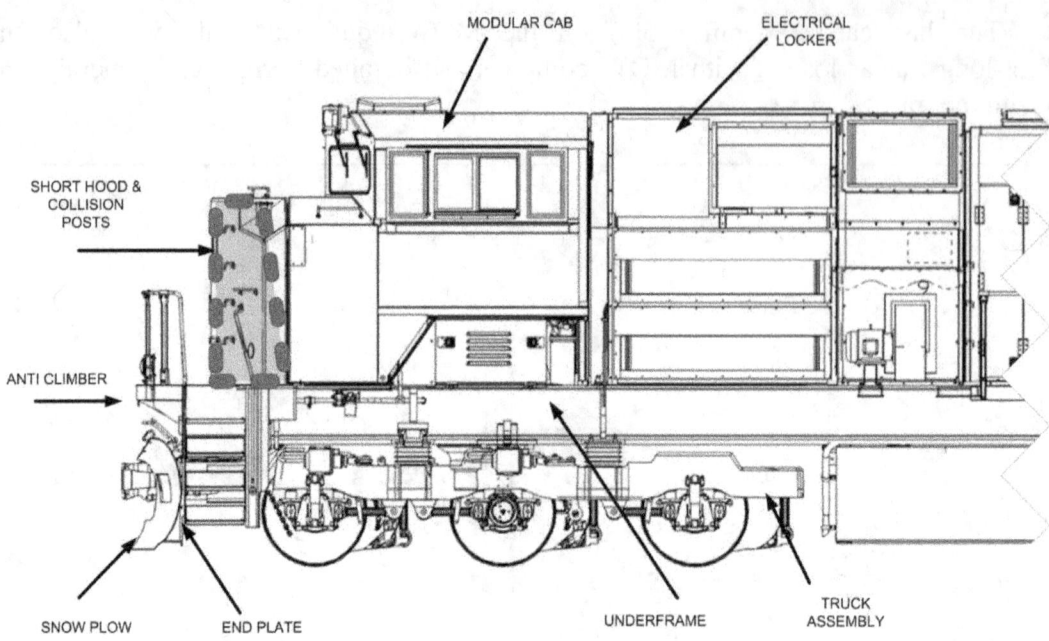

MODULAR CAB

ELECTRICAL LOCKER

SHORT HOOD & COLLISION POSTS

ANTI CLIMBER

SNOW PLOW   END PLATE   UNDERFRAME   TRUCK ASSEMBLY

Figure 10. Side view of front end of EMD SD70ACe locomotive, the same type of locomotive as striking train lead locomotive, BNSF 9159.

The modular cab of the locomotive sustained a substantial loss of occupied space. The cab was separated from the deck of the locomotive, and the bottom half of the cab rotated up just over 90 degrees. (See figure 11.) The cab was crushed at the rooftop, and the left rear corner of the cab was crushed in. The side walls remained intact to the point of the window line, which is about 4 feet from the roof. The underside of the cab was relatively intact and undamaged. The entire cab had extensive fire exposure and damage.

Figure 11. Upended striking train locomotive (BNSF 9159) modular operating cab.

The rear of the cab module abuts the electrical locker. The general condition of the electrical locker indicated that it had been subjected to severe longitudinal forces, and it was crushed at the upper right side. The locker became separated from the floor mounting system and was pushed back more than 2 feet.

The interior of the cab was severely damaged by fire.[12] The general condition of the modular cab attachment fixtures indicated that they had been subjected to severe vertical forces and shear. The rear posts were broken along the welds that hold the cylindrical posts to the deck. The forward-mounted floor brackets had indications of deep scoring on the inboard sides in a manner consistent with vertical loading. The modular cab assembly was examined, revealing the remaining volume of survivable space to be an estimated 65 cubic feet. Both the engineer's and the conductor's sides of the cab were severely damaged and burned. The engineer's seat was sheared from the floor mounts, and the control panel was bent downward and inward. The conductor's seat remained attached, and the desk area was crushed toward the floor.

---

[12] The flatcars that overrode the locomotive carried MOW equipment with diesel fuel tanks.

The 5000-gallon fuel tank mounted to the underframe at the bottom plate was not compromised. The left side of the tank had minor scraping along the sidewall.

The second locomotive on the striking coal train, BNSF 6133, also derailed but stayed upright and generally in line with the track. Collision damage was much less severe and involved primarily raking damage along the right (north) side from the derailed flatcars and the MOW equipment from the cars. The diesel fuel tank on BNSF 6133 was punctured on the right rear corner of the sidewall/end plate, and leaking diesel fuel caught fire.

The first two loaded coal cars (cars 1–2) derailed upright and came to rest in line with the track. These two cars and the next seven (cars 3–9) were damaged by raking action along their sides from derailed cars and freight.

1.3   Personnel Information

1.3.1 Engineer of Striking Train

The 48-year-old engineer was hired by the BNSF on July 14, 1997. His seniority date as an engineer was March 15, 1999. He had passed rules examinations on a regular basis and was current in his engineer's certification. His most recent recertification was on July 10, 2008. Other than three brief periods in Kansas City, Missouri, and once in Lincoln, Nebraska, he had primarily worked out of Creston, Iowa, since May 2003. He had five disciplinary actions on his record including one for excessive speed and another related to noncompliance with Form B[13] track bulletin requirements. The other three disciplinary actions were considered less serious and involved train handling and absenteeism. The engineer had been placed on an employee review process (ERP)[14] on March 11, 2009. He was in the ERP program at the time of the accident. The engineer's supervisor told investigators that the engineer's performance had improved and that he was a candidate for removal from the program.

1.3.2 Conductor of Striking Train

The 48-year-old conductor was hired as a brakeman by the BNSF on November 22, 2004. Her seniority date as an engineer was January 21, 2007. She was certified as a locomotive engineer but was working as a conductor. Her seniority date as a

---

[13] Form B track bulletins are issued to establish work zones on the right-of-way.

[14] The BNSF ERP is intended to help employees work the remainder of their careers without an accident or injury. When an employee's record indicates that individual assistance is needed, the supervisor contacts the employee and conducts an ERP session. Criteria for selection of employees for the ERP include injury history, human factor rail equipment incidents, operations testing failures, new employees with incidents or injuries, and supervisor awareness of performance concern. Employees in this program are tested more frequently on train operations, have their event recorder tapes reviewed, and meet with their supervisors on a regular basis.

conductor was March 14, 2005. She had one disciplinary action on her record: "Excess speed in restricted speed." At the time of this event, she was working as a conductor.

1.3.3 Work-Rest Cycles of Crew of Striking Train

Both the engineer and the conductor were called for duty on Sunday, April 17, 2011, at 1:01 a.m., and they went on duty at 2:31 a.m. (the accident trip) in Lincoln, Nebraska. They both had been off duty for 12 hours 1 minute and had stayed at an away-from-home lodging facility provided by the railroad.

The day before the accident (Saturday, April 16), the engineer was called for duty at 3:02 a.m.; went on duty at 4:30 a.m.; traveled from Creston, Iowa, to Lincoln, Nebraska; and went off duty at 2:30 p.m. Between April 11 and April 15, he had marked off (taken himself off) the call list for union business and for taking an engineer recertification examination. Also on Saturday, April 16, the conductor was called for duty at 3:00 a.m.; went on duty at 4:30 a.m.; traveled from Creston, Iowa, to Lincoln, Nebraska; and went off duty at 2:30 p.m. On Friday, April 15, the conductor was on duty from 2:25 a.m. to 2:10 p.m. On Thursday, April 14, she worked from 3:10 a.m. to 1:10 p.m.

1.3.4 Engineer of Struck Train

The 43-year-old engineer was hired in 1994 as a conductor trainee. Since April 16, 1995, he had worked as an engineer. His engineer certification was current.

1.3.5 Conductor of Struck Train

The 26-year-old conductor was hired by the BNSF on February 2, 2004. His seniority date as a locomotive engineer is August 6, 2006.

1.3.6 Work-Rest Cycles of Crew of Struck Train

The engineer was called for duty on April 17, 2011, in Lincoln, Nebraska, at 12:05 a.m. and went on duty for the accident trip at 1:15 a.m. The day before the accident (Saturday, April 16), he was called at 12:31 a.m.; went on duty at 2:00 a.m.; traveled from Creston, Iowa, to Lincoln, Nebraska; and went off duty at 1:45 p.m. The day before (Friday, April 15) he had the day off. The engineer had been off duty from April 11 through April 15.

The conductor also was called for duty for the accident trip on Sunday, April 17, 2011, in Lincoln, Nebraska, at 12:05 a.m. and went on duty at 1:15 a.m. The day before (Saturday, April 16) he was called at 12:30 a.m., went on duty at 2:15 a.m., and traveled from Creston, Iowa, to Lincoln, Nebraska. He went off duty at 1:45 p.m. and stayed at a local hotel. On Thursday, April 14, he was called at 8:21 p.m. and went on duty at 9:50 p.m. He was on duty until 10:15 a.m. on Friday, April 15.

1.4   Track and Site Information

The Creston Subdivision is located on the Nebraska Division and begins at Creston, Iowa, and continues westward to Lincoln, Nebraska. (See figure 12.) The railroad in the vicinity of the accident is multiple main track territory. The maximum timetable speed on the Creston Subdivision is 60 mph for freight trains, 79 mph for passenger trains, and 45 mph for trains exceeding 100 TPOB.

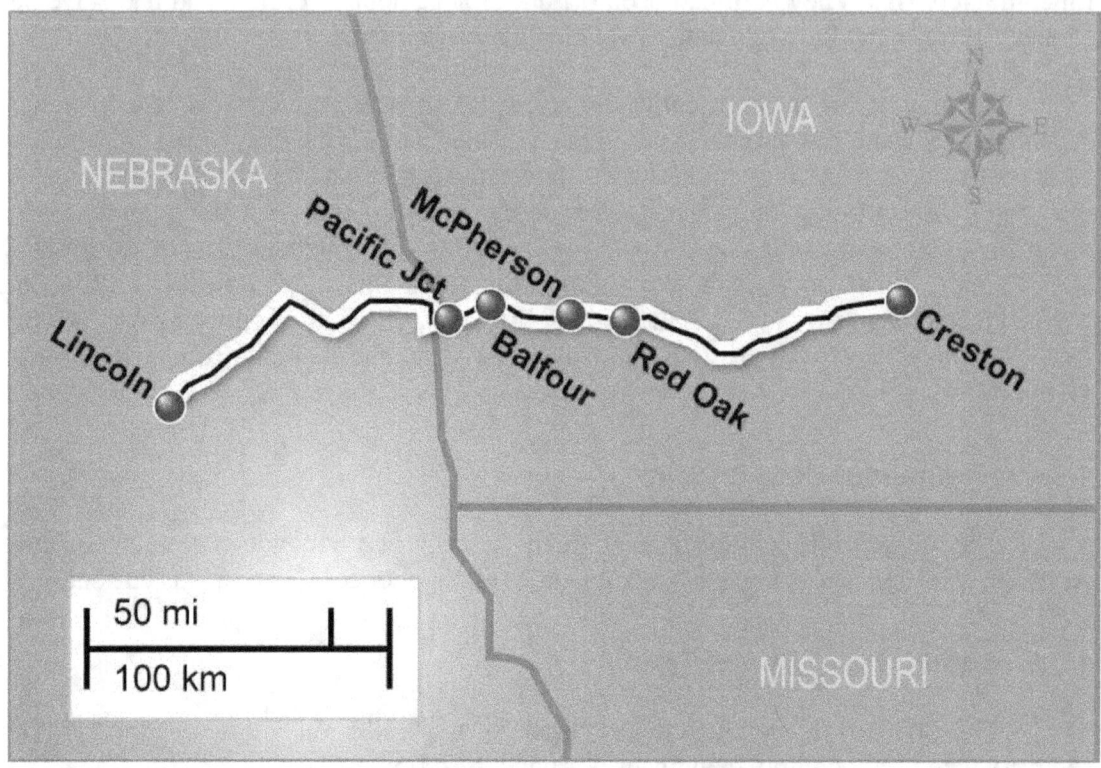

Figure 12. Creston subdivision of BNSF Nebraska division.

There are two main tracks at the accident site. The bulk of the train traffic in that area is made up of coal trains. Loaded coal trains travel east from the Powder River Basin to various utility power plants in the midwest and east; empty coal trains move west. Generally, loaded coal trains are routed on track two, as was the case in this accident. Other freight trains also operate on this route as do Amtrak trains. Amtrak passenger trains No. 5 and No. 6[15] operate daily, connecting Chicago with the San Francisco Bay area.

The collision occurred near the east end of a 10.6-mile length of parallel tracks between CP 4580 and CP McPherson. There are crossovers near the midpoint at CP 4535. (See figure 2.)

---

[15] Amtrak No. 5 operates westbound; No. 6 operates eastbound.

1.5   Method of Operations

Train operations on this portion of the BNSF were governed and authorized by traffic control system signal indications under the control of a train dispatcher located at the Network Operations Center (NOC) in Fort Worth, Texas. Train dispatchers at the NOC set routes at each control point that establish the priorities for, and control, train movements. Typically, intermediate signals are positioned between control points that govern the use of discrete signal blocks. At the accident site there were two main tracks, each signaled for train movements in both directions.

The crews were governed by the General Code of Operating Rules (GCOR),[16] Sixth Edition, effective April 7, 2010. The territory was designated the BNSF Nebraska Division, Creston Subdivision. At the time of the accident, the current timetable was Nebraska Division Timetable No. 7, effective May 12, 2010.

Intermediate signals are located on both main tracks at MP 450.38 about midway between the crossovers at CP 4535 (MP 453.4) and CP McPherson (MP 447.5). The last signal the striking coal train passed before the accident was intermediate signal 24504.[17] This consisted of a three-position color-light display with a G plate[18] and a number plate attached to the signal mast. (See figure 13.) Signal system data indicated that this signal was displaying a red (restricting) aspect. There were no slow orders, track bulletins, or other advisories in effect between the grade signal and the point of collision.

No speed or stop signal enforcement (positive train control system) is installed in this area. The locomotive engineer is responsible for train speed management and stopping at appropriate locations in accordance with operating rules and signal indications.

1.5.1   Grade Signal Description

GCOR rule 9.1.13, *Signal Aspects and Indications*, illustrates many signal aspects that are called "restricting," including flashing red, lunar, and a solid red intermediate signal with a G plate and a number plate attached to the mast. For all these signal aspects, their indication is "proceed at restricted speed." When a train encounters an intermediate signal displaying a red aspect and that has a G plate, the train is not required to stop but must reduce speed to restricted speed before passing the signal. The GCOR restricted speed rule (Rule 6.27, *Movement at Restricted Speed*) is quoted below:

---

[16] The GCOR is a standard book of operating rules used by many railroads in the United States. It was developed by a committee composed of railroads that adopted the GCOR, and it is updated periodically by the committee. Each railroad that adopts the GCOR remains free to modify specific rules to better suit its individual operating characteristics.

[17] Signals between control points are called *intermediate signals*. These signals provide information about the track ahead but do not convey movement authority.

[18] A *G plate* is a small sign reading "G" that is attached to a signal mast. The G stands for grade; signals are located on grades where it is prudent to avoid stopping a train on an upgrade because restarting may be difficult and result in a stall or a break in two.

When required to move at restricted speed, movement must be made at a speed that allows stopping within half the range of vision short of:

- Train.

- Engine.

- Railroad car.

- Men or equipment fouling the track.

- Stop signal.

Or

- Derail or switch lined improperly.

When a train or engine is required to move at restricted speed, the crew must keep a lookout for broken rail and not exceed 20 [mph].

Comply with these requirements until the leading wheels reach a point where movement at restricted speed is no longer required.

Figure 13. Eastbound intermediate grade signal 24504 with G Plate.

1.6   Train Information

The striking coal train consisted of 130 loaded coal cars, weighed 18,529 tons, and was 7,122 feet long. It had two locomotives on the head end and one locomotive on the rear end.[19] The struck MOW equipment train consisted of 21 loaded cars and 13 empty cars, weighed 2,635 tons, and was 3,170 feet long with one locomotive on the head end. The rear portion of the train included flatcars with various types of self-powered MOW equipment as cargo.

1.6.1 Striking Train Locomotives

BNSF 9159. The lead locomotive of the striking train, BNSF 9159, was an Electro-Motive Diesel (EMD) SD70ACe manufactured in March 2008. (See figures 14 and 15.) This unit is a six-axle, two-truck,[20] 4300-horsepower, diesel-electric locomotive. The locomotive measures about 74 feet long, 10 feet wide, and 16 feet high. It weighs about 420,000 pounds. The design incorporates a modular operator's cab at the front end of the unit and has a fabricated steel underframe that extends the length of the unit, upon which the diesel engine and alternator components are mounted (aft of the operator's cab).

The modular cab is bolted in place at its rear floor underside on two hollow cylindrical posts about 10 inches in diameter that are welded to the top plate of the locomotive. Welded atop these sections are square plates, or flanges, on which the rear section of the cab is bolted. The two rear cab mounting points are fitted with torsional bushings that establish a pivot point about the rear floor axis of the cab.

The front of the modular cab rests on two coil springs located behind the short hood about 5 feet 10 inches above the underframe top plate behind the short hood. Adjustment cups at each spring are used to control the clearance from cab to underframe and to equalize spring compression. Adjacent to each spring are hydraulic shock absorbers designed to dampen vibrations.

---

[19] This configuration of locomotives (two in front/one on rear) is commonly referred to as distributed power. The locomotive engineer in the lead locomotive typically controls all of the distributed power locomotives in the train, and this was the case at Red Oak.

[20] Wheel-axle sets are held in place in frames, and these assemblies are referred to as trucks.

Figure 14. Illustration of EMD SD70Ace locomotive (same type as striking train locomotive) with white boxes indicating the points where the isolated cab attaches to the underframe.

On the underside of the modular cab at its front are two double shear pin joints. This system includes two brackets welded to the top plate and two brackets welded to the underside of the cab floor. These joints are designed as a clearance fit;[21] a 1-inch-diameter hardened steel pin passes through a wide (2-inch) hole in the deck-mounted bracket. When questioned, EMD stated that this design acted as a loosely coupled fastening system.

Other fixtures include stinger assemblies, or oversized turnbuckles, and dampers. These additional fixtures limit the lateral motion of the operating cab assembly sitting on the deck of the locomotive.

---

[21] A *clearance fit* provides clearance between a shaft and a hole and permits relative freedom of motion of the two—axially, radially, or both.

Figure 15. Exemplar EMD SD70ACe locomotive (same type as striking train locomotive) with modular cab.

A fuel tank with a capacity of about 5,000 gallons is located (suspended from the underframe) between the truck assemblies.

BNSF 9159 was built following a crashworthiness design standard prescribed in the Association of American Railroads (AAR) *Manual of Standards and Recommended Practices*, Standard S-580, revised 2005. AAR Standard S-580 is incorporated by reference in Title 49 *Code of Federal Regulations* (CFR) 229.225 for all locomotives built after January 2009. Selected design requirements in Standard S-580, for wide-nose locomotives, are listed below:

- Impact-resistant fuel tank

- Underframe designed to withstand a longitudinal load of 1 million pounds

- Collision posts

- Anti-climbers designed to withstand a vertical force of 100,000 pounds

AAR Standard S-580 also includes crashworthiness requirements for other types of locomotives, including narrow-nose locomotives. For narrow-nose locomotives, the standard includes crashworthiness requirements for operator cab corner posts, but S-580 does not contain such requirements for wide-nose locomotives. AAR Standard S-580 does not contain any criteria related to operating cabs—conventional[22] or modular (isolated)—for wide-nose locomotives. Additionally, BNSF 9159 was constructed to meet fuel tank performance standards prescribed in AAR Standard S-5506, revised 2001, "Performance Requirements for Diesel Electric Locomotive Fuel Tanks," which is a standard incorporated by reference in 49 CFR 229.205.

BNSF 6133. The second locomotive of the striking train, BNSF 6133, was a General Electric ES44AC built in November 2006. This unit is a six-axle, two-truck, 4400-horsepower, diesel-electric locomotive. The crew cab on this model locomotive (unoccupied at the time of the accident) is of nonmodular design.

BNSF 6133 measures about 73 feet long, 10 feet wide, and 15 1/2 feet high, and it weighs about 415,000 pounds. A fuel tank with a capacity of about 5,000 gallons is located (suspended from the underside of the underframe) between the truck assemblies. BNSF 6133 also was manufactured to AAR S-580 crashworthiness standards and S-5506 fuel tank performance standards in effect at the time of manufacture.

1.6.2 Last 10 Cars on Struck Train

The last car of the struck train, the 34th car, was the HZGX-150, a clip car. (See figure 16.) This was the first car struck by locomotive BNSF 9159 in the collision. It is a diesel-engine-powered self-propelled unit that can be coupled into a train for transport. It has a 300-gallon fuel tank. This car was manufactured by Herzog Railroad Services, Inc.; weighed 177,000 pounds; and was 54 feet long.[23]

---

[22] A *conventional* operating cab is permanently attached to the supporting frame of the locomotive, thus becoming a single unit.

[23] Information from Universal Machine Language Equipment Register, or UMLER.

Figure 16. Exemplar HZGX clip car.

The second to the last car in the struck train was BNSF 927022. This was a scorpion car: an 89-foot flatcar with a folding loading ramp attached to the end of the car. (See figure 17.) The scorpion ramp was composed of six segments tied together with pin joints and hydraulic rams. The ramp unfolds so that MOW equipment can roll on and off the flatcar. When the ramp is fully open and extended, it is 52 feet 8 inches long. The ramp is powered by a diesel engine and has an 11.5-gallon fuel tank. The hydraulic fluid tank had a 25-gallon capacity. This car weighed 155,400 pounds.

Figure 17. Exemplar scorpion-equipped flatcar.

The next eight derailed cars in the MOW equipment train were 89-foot-long flatcars with MOW equipment secured to them as cargo.

1.7   Meteorological Information

On April 17 at 6:55 a.m., the weather at Red Oak Airport, which is about 3 1/2 miles east of the accident site, was reported as misty with a temperature of 30° F and visibility of 5 miles. The accident occurred in daylight; sunrise that day was at 6:40 a.m. The crew of the struck train described the visibility in the area as good at the time of the collision.

1.8   Medical Information

1.8.1   Striking Train Engineer

The BNSF medical records for the engineer of the striking coal train indicated that his most recent hearing and vision tests were on March 21, 2011. Although the hearing test indicated that he had some loss of hearing in both ears for high-pitched sounds (that is, whistles, birds, some speech sounds), he still met the Federal Railroad Administration (FRA) hearing acuity requirements in 49 CFR 240.121. His vision examination indicated that he did not wear glasses for distance or reading and his color vision was normal.

NTSB investigators obtained the engineer's medical records from his personal physician. His last visit to this physician was on May 6, 2009. On that date, he weighed 228 pounds and he was about 67 inches tall. His body mass index (BMI)[24] was 35.7. He had had Type 2 diabetes for several years and had been prescribed repaglinide; glyburide and metformin; and pioglitazone.[25] He had been prescribed valsartan for high blood pressure. He also had been prescribed ezetimibe and simvastatin, and rosuvastatin, for high cholesterol. (See appendix D for medications discussed in this report and their indications.) There was no indication in the records provided that he had undergone a sleep study.

1.8.2   Striking Train Conductor

The conductor's BNSF medical records indicated that she had sustained an injury on November 4, 2010 (and was subsequently out of service for several months). These records also indicated that she had "impingement problem shoulder" and that she required surgery. The BNSF records indicated she could return to work, to full duty with

---

[24] Body mass index is a relationship between weight and height that is associated with body fat and health risk. BMI is calculated by dividing weight in kilograms by height in meters squared. Obesity is defined as a BMI of 30 and above. (Source: National Institutes of Health)

[25] Repaglinide; glyburide and metformin; and pioglitazone are medications prescribed to treat Type 2 diabetes.

no restrictions, on March 18, 2011. The November 4, 2010, records also indicated that she was regularly taking valsartan for high blood pressure and pramipexole for restless legs syndrome. She returned to work on March 21, 2011, and had been released to full unrestricted duty. Her hearing tests conducted on May 5, 2010, indicated that her hearing was normal. She passed her vision test on April 3, 2009.

NTSB investigators obtained the conductor's medical records from her personal physician. Investigators also noted various medications that were recovered from her locker after the accident. The following information is based on information from these two sources.

The conductor's medical records indicated that she was 64 1/4 inches tall and weighed 221 pounds on November 8, 2010. Her BMI was 37.6. She was noted to be hypertensive on November 8, 2010, with a blood pressure of 140/88. The records indicated that she was being treated for high blood pressure with both metoprolol and valsartan. In addition, she was being treated for restless legs syndrome with ropinirole, an anti-Parkinson's disease medication. Medications found in her locker included temazepam (used to treat insomnia), which had been prescribed on March 9, 2011. She also had diphenhydramine, an over-the-counter sedating antihistamine, in her locker. Her medical records indicated that she had been prescribed venlafaxine (an antidepressant). Her snoring history was not available. There was no indication in the records provided that she had undergone a sleep study.

1.8.3 Toxicological Information

In accordance with Federal regulations, the engineer and the conductor of the struck train were required to provide postaccident blood and urine specimens, which they did at a hospital in Creston, Iowa. The Montgomery County, Iowa, coroner collected specimens from the engineer and the conductor of the striking train. The specimens from crewmembers of both trains were negative for illegal drugs and ingested alcohol.

NTSB investigators requested additional toxicological analyses on the striking train crew's specimens be conducted at the Civil Aeronautical Medical Institute in Oklahoma City, Oklahoma. The conductor's toxicological results showed that valsartan (a prescription medication used to treat high blood pressure) had been detected in the urine and the blood. Results for the engineer showed that chlorpheniramine (used to treat symptoms related to allergies and the common cold) had been found in the urine but not in the blood. In addition, ranitidine (used to treat ulcers and gastroesophageal reflux disease, also known as GERD) was found in both his blood and his urine.

The Montgomery County coroner conducted autopsies on the two crewmembers of the striking coal train. The toxicological analysis of the engineer's heart blood revealed ranitidine, 100 ng/mL, and caffeine. The autopsy report concluded that he died of "blunt force injuries to the head and thermal injuries." The toxicological analysis of the conductor's heart blood revealed no detectable concentrations of drugs on a comprehensive drug panel. The only positive result was for caffeine. The report concluded that the cause of death was "blunt force injuries of the head." The report also stated, "Other significant: thermal injuries." The coroner also conducted toxicological tests for the presence of carbon monoxide on both crewmembers on the striking train, and these tests were negative.

1.9 Tests and Research

1.9.1 Postaccident Signal System Inspection and Testing

Investigators conducted postaccident field inspections and testing of the signal system. The inspections found no indications of tampering or vandalism that would interfere with the operation of the signal system. Relay positions were found to be in accordance with the physical location of the accident trains and the displayed signal aspects. Investigators did not identify any exceptions with either the design or the operation of the signal system. Minor signal system damage was observed as a result of the collision.

Investigators collected and reviewed BNSF signal system maintenance records for the accident area. The records indicated that all signal tests and inspections had been conducted in accordance with BNSF requirements and Federal regulations. Signal trouble reports for the previous 3 months were also reviewed, and no exceptions were noted.

1.9.2 Track

The two main tracks at the accident site are generally parallel and run east and west. The northern track is designated track one, and the southern track is track two. On both tracks, 136-pound continuous welded rail was laid on wood ties set in ballast and held in place with spikes and tie plates. Annual traffic on track two totals 94 million gross tons and on track one, 23 million gross tons. Visual inspection of track in the accident area did not reveal any anomalies except those associated with damage from the collision and derailment.

1.9.3 Mechanical Tests and Inspections

On the morning of April 18, 2011, investigators inspected all the cars of the striking coal train where they came to rest. Three minor exceptions were noted, none of which could have prevented train brakes from applying. To test the brakes, the brake pipe was charged to 90 pounds per square inch (psi), and after the air had equalized, a 20-psi brake application was made. The brakes on all 130 cars applied as designed.

Maintenance Records. A review of the maintenance and inspection records for the lead locomotive on the striking train (BNSF 9159) indicated that all the required FRA and BNSF inspections were current. There were no unrepaired defects that would have rendered the unit unfit for service including exhaust fumes leaking into the control compartment.

Locomotive Control Positions. The leading locomotive of the striking train sustained severe crush and thermal damage during the collision and subsequent fire. The control positions on the engineer's side of the operating compartment could not be physically verified. There was also extensive damage on the conductor's side, but investigators were able to observe that the conductor's emergency brake valve had not been activated. Locomotive event recorder data also indicated that the conductor's emergency brake valve had not been activated before impact.

Preaccident Inspections. BNSF records indicate that on the morning of the accident, BNSF car inspectors completed the required brake tests and mechanical inspections on the striking coal train at Lincoln, Nebraska, with no defects reported.

Metallurgical Examinations - Forward Cab Retention Pins. Investigators from the NTSB's Materials Laboratory conducted a postaccident examination of locomotive BNSF 9159 in Havelock, Nebraska. Pieces of the two forward cab retention pins were taken to the NTSB laboratory in Washington, D.C., for further examination. The retention pins are part of the loosely coupled fastening system of the isolated operating cab on the EMD SD70ACe locomotive as described in section 1.6.1 of this report.

Both retention pins were fractured through the thickness about midway along the shank. The fracture features on both pins were consistent with overstress of surface-hardened steel under a bending load.

The retention pin dimensions were within the EMD-specified tolerances. The metallurgical composition of the pins was evaluated, and the material was identified as carbon steel; manganese levels were within the compositional ranges of the carbon steels that EMD specified for this part. Hardness values were generally consistent with the specified material, although surface hardness was slightly below specification in one pin that showed evidence of heat damage.

1.9.4 Sight-Distance Observations

Investigators conducted sight-distance observations to determine the visibility of the two signals leading up to the accident site and to examine the visibility of the rear clip car of the standing train. The weather conditions during these observations were similar to those described by the crew of the struck train at the time of the accident. The signals were set to display the same aspects (yellow approach at CP 4535, red restricting at intermediate grade signal 24504) as were displayed to the striking train. An exemplar clip car was positioned on the curve at the point of collision with an end-of-train device attached.[26] Observers were positioned in the cab of a locomotive of the same type as BNSF 9159. The observation locomotive was operated by a BNSF engineer who regularly works this territory. He was instructed to note the location where he could clearly see the yellow approach signal at CP 4535, the red restricting signal 24504, and the standing clip car. Observers then confirmed these locations. The observations were conducted within an hour of the time of day that the accident had occurred. Sight-distance measurements were taken from the locomotive distance counter. Table 2 lists the distances recorded during these observations.

During the sight-distance observations, investigators were stationed at various signal locations to observe signal displays while the test train traversed the accident area. No anomalies were observed.

Table 2. Sight-distance observations.

Observable Feature	Distance Observed (feet)
Yellow approach signal at CP 4535	4658
Red restricting grade signal 24504	3147
Exemplar clip car placed at point of impact	1364

1.9.5 Cellular Telephone Use

Investigators obtained the cellular phone records of the engineers and the conductors of both the struck train and the striking train. These records indicated that the crewmembers of both trains were not using their cell phones for verbal communication or for texting during the accident trips.

While off duty on April 16, 2011, the engineer of the striking train made several outgoing calls, the majority of them between 3:51 and 4:17 p.m. The last call he made that day using his cell phone was at 6:46 p.m. There was no record of any calls made by the conductor on the day before the accident.

1.9.6 Event Recorders

Railroad Signal Event Recorders. Investigators collected information from the event recorders at four signal locations: CP McPherson; intermediate grade signal 24504; CP 4535; and the BNSF NOC in Fort Worth, Texas. An examination of the signal data was conducted with no exceptions noted.

---

[26] An end-of-train device is mounted on the rear of the rear car of a train and is connected to the air brake system. It provides information to the engineer about air brake system pressure. It is also reflective and has a flashing light controlled by a photo cell In the Red Oak accident, the flashing light was not operating at the time of the collision because of the amount of ambient light.

Locomotive Event Recorders. The locomotive on the struck train and the three locomotives on the striking train were all equipped with event recorders. Data from the struck train was downloaded and reviewed on scene. The data confirmed that the train was stopped at the time of collision and that the collision forces moved the locomotive forward about 17 feet. Data from the event recorders from the second and third locomotives on the striking train also were downloaded and reviewed on scene.

On board the lead locomotive on the striking train, BNSF 9159, was a functionally integrated railroad equipment (FIRE) computer that monitored and recorded a number of operating parameters including those required by FRA event recorder regulations in 49 CFR 229.135. The FIRE computer also controlled the in-cab operating displays viewed by the locomotive engineer. Event recorder data were simultaneously stored in the FIRE computer memory and on a hard drive in a certified[27] U.S. Department of Transportation crashworthy event recorder memory module. (See figure 18.) Because of extensive collision and fire damage to the lead locomotive, the FIRE computer on BNSF 9159 was destroyed. However, although it had been damaged by fire, the crashworthy event recorder memory module was recovered and shipped to the NTSB laboratory in Washington, D.C. (See figure 19.) The crash-hardened memory module case was opened, and the memory board was removed. Event recorder data were downloaded directly from the memory board to a computer.

---

[27] Title 49 CFR 229.135 requires that the manufacturer, in this case Bach-Simpson, certify that the memory module meets standards contained in Appendix D to Part 229.

Figure 18. Intact exemplar crashworthy event recorder memory module.

Figure 19. Fire-damaged memory module recovered from BNSF 9159.

Locomotive Cab Video Recorders. The lead locomotive of the striking train, BNSF 9159, had a Wabtec Video Trax model forward-facing video recorder. The recorder hard drive enclosure was located in the wreckage, successfully recovered, and shipped to the NTSB laboratory in Washington, D.C. The enclosure and its contents were in poor condition because of the fire. (See figures 20 and 21.) Video data is stored on a hard drive within the enclosure. The hard drive was removed and transported to a vendor specializing in hard drive data recovery. After an examination and attempts to repair the damaged hard drive, it was determined that the hard drive was damaged beyond repair and its contents were unrecoverable. Forward-facing video recorders are not required by regulation.

Figure 20. Exemplar video recorder hard drive enclosure (orange case).

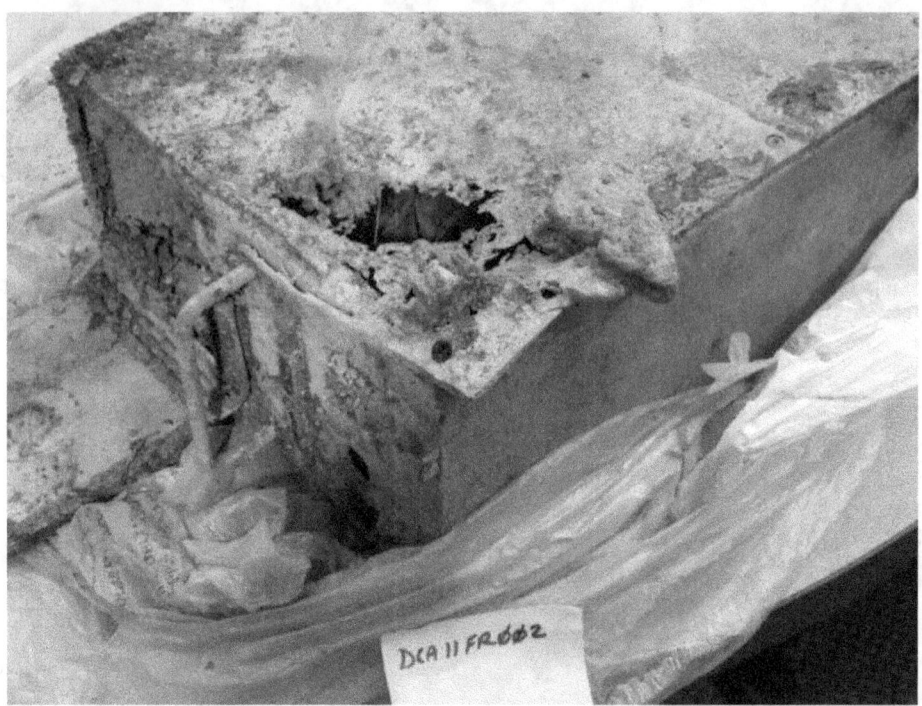

Figure 21. Fire-damaged video recorder hard drive enclosure from
BNSF 9159.

1.9.7 Emergency Response

The Montgomery County Sheriff's emergency dispatch logs indicate that a 911 call reporting the collision was received at 6:57 a.m. Six additional 911 calls reporting the collision were received over the next few minutes including a call from the BNSF NOC at 7:03 a.m. At that time, BNSF train traffic was suspended through the accident area. Emergency dispatch logs show that the first fire unit arrived at 7:10 a.m.

Investigators interviewed the Red Oak fire chief, who served as incident commander (IC), and a volunteer firefighter, who served as liaison officer with the BNSF. The IC said that the emergency responders' first contact on scene was with the crew of the struck train, who said that the two crewmembers on the striking train may have jumped before the impact. A thorough search of the area, conducted by three different teams, did not locate either crewmember.

The IC described first encountering diesel fires in three areas: (1) at the front of the lead locomotive of the striking train, (2) at the second locomotive of the striking train, and (3) at the Herzog clip car that had been struck in the collision, near the point of collision (the fire fed by a large diesel fuel tank). He described a small leak from the fuel tank of BNSF 9159[28] and a much larger leak from the fuel tank on BNSF 6133.[29] He also noted evidence of a flash fire on the west side of the highway overpass.

The IC reported that it took about 2 hours to fully extinguish all the fires. Fire suppression began about 7:15 a.m., using 50 gallons of class A foam[30] at 1.5 percent concentration. (See figure 22.) A supply of class B foam arrived on scene about 30 minutes into the response, and 150 gallons were consumed at 3 percent concentration. Fire suppression was complete about 9:15 a.m.

Figure 22. Red Oak Fire Department applying foam after collision.

The Red Oak Fire Department (ROFD) liaison officer indicated that cooperation, communication, and support from the BNSF were "very good." Safety briefings were

---

[28] A detailed postaccident examination of the BNSF 9159 did not reveal a breach in the fuel tank. There were a number of damaged diesel tanks from the MOW equipment on the flatcars that may have fed this fire.

[29] Postaccident examination of BNSF 6133 confirmed a fuel tank breach. See section 1.2.6, "Wreckage," in this report.

[30] Class A foam is designed for fires of combustible material. Class B foam is designed for flammable liquid fires.

held at appropriate points during the course of the emergency response, and BNSF personnel were responsive with information and resources.

The IC reported that the pileup of cars and equipment on top of BNSF locomotive 9159 was judged to be too precarious and unsafe for ROFD personnel to attempt to reach the location of the crew's bodies. The BNSF's contractor was tasked with removing and/or shoring up equipment to make access safe.

During removal of one of the last railroad cars from on top of BNSF 9159, the cab module was displaced and ended up on the south side of the locomotive. When the cab module was stabilized, hydraulic rams were used to open the skylight area of the roof of the cab module to provide access to the cab. The bodies of the striking train's crew were located about 4:09 p.m. and were removed about 4:38 p.m. The IC led the recovery team and indicated that the cab roof was crushed to the tops of the seats and there was open space between the floor and the seat tops. The crew's bodies were transported to Ankeny, Iowa, for autopsy following the Montgomery County coroner's instructions.

The IC reported that the ROFD had participated in annual training with the BNSF and that he felt the ROFD was well prepared for a response to a railroad accident of this type. He noted that based on prior familiarization training, he was able to shut down the diesel engine on the second locomotive, BNSF 6133, that was still idling when the ROFD arrived at the scene.

No emergency responders were injured during this incident.

1.9.8 Other Information

Locomotive Crashworthiness and Fuel Tank Standards. In 1997 the FRA tasked the Railroad Safety Advisory Committee (RSAC)[31] to "investigate and develop, if necessary, crashworthiness specifications to ensure the integrity of the locomotive cab in accidents resulting from collisions such as highway-rail crossing accidents, sideswipes, and shifted loads."[32] RSAC reviewed accident data from 1995 to 1996 and resolved the data pool into 23 types of accidents. Of these 23 types, RSAC selected five accident scenarios that encompassed the range of collisions that it believed the FRA intended for the investigation of crashworthiness specifications. The scenarios included the following:

- In-line collision involving a train with two locomotives in the lead in which the second locomotive overrides the lead (the first) locomotive

- In-line head-on collision of two trains in which one opposing locomotive overrides the other

---

[31] Established by the FRA in 1996, RSAC provides a forum for consensus rulemaking. Representatives include railroads, labor organizations, suppliers, state agencies, and manufacturers.

[32] FRA RSAC Task 97-1.

- Grade-crossing collision with a highway vehicle hauling logs in which the principal impact is on the window area of the locomotive

- Oblique collision of a locomotive with an intermodal trailer

- Oblique collision of a locomotive with a freight car

Many modifications to the design of locomotives were investigated, tested, and compared with baseline locomotive designs. The modifications included shelf couplers, anti-climbers, modified collision posts, and increased strength of the window structure and the short hood. The modifications deemed most likely to improve locomotive integrity were strengthened window structures, collision posts, and short hoods, depending on the collision scenario.

The AAR S-580 standard provides crashworthiness design criteria for all new locomotives used in occupied service and requires specific features to be incorporated into the equipment, such as underframe strength, collision post strength, anti-climbers on each end, emergency egress, and emergency lighting and interior requirements.

The AAR S-5506 standard provides performance design criteria for all locomotives equipped with external fuel tanks and requires specific features to be incorporated into the design, such as structural strength requirements to improve crashworthiness in the event of minor derailments, a jackknifed locomotive, side impact collisions, and sideswipes, and to resist penetration and control spills.

The FRA adopted both AAR S-580 and AAR S-5506 as regulatory requirements[33] in a final rule on August 28, 2006. No locomotives with modular type crew cabs were in service at that time.

Positive Train Control: BNSF Railway Electronic Train Management System. Positive train control (PTC) refers to technology that is capable of preventing train-to-train collisions, overspeed derailments, movement through an improperly lined switch, and injuries to or the deaths of workers on the right-of-way within work zones resulting from unauthorized train incursions. PTC systems vary widely in complexity and sophistication based on their level of automation and functionality, their system architecture, the wayside system upon which they are based (for example, non-signaled, block signal, cab signal), and their degree of train control.

Before October 2008, various railroads were voluntarily installing PTC systems. However, the Rail Safety Improvement Act of 2008 (RSIA)[34] mandated the widespread installation of PTC systems by December 31, 2015.

---

[33] 49 CFR 229.205 and 229.217.

[34] Signed on October 16, 2008, as Public Law 110-432.

Currently, all affected railroads are pursuing the development and implementation of PTC in accordance with their PTC implementation plans, which are required by the RSIA, and that have been approved by the FRA. Railroads are adapting their individual PTC systems to maximize interoperability.[35] The BNSF Railway, Union Pacific Railroad, Norfolk Southern Railway, and CSX Transportation are leading the interoperability effort with technology based on the Electronic Train Management System (ETMS) for rail traffic outside of the Northeast Corridor. Amtrak is undertaking a similar effort for rail traffic in the Northeast Corridor using the Advanced Civil Speed Enforcement System.

The FRA has issued regulatory requirements for PTC systems on railroads that fall under RSIA as well as rail carriers that are continuing to implement PTC voluntarily. The FRA is also providing support through a combination of project safety oversight, technology development, and financial assistance.

The BNSF has received FRA approval for full revenue deployment of its ETMS Version 1 on 35 subdivisions and has received type approval and system certification for the use of ETMS Version 6. The BNSF and the FRA are working together on testing a further enhanced version of ETMS on additional subdivisions, taking an incremental development step toward interoperability.

The ETMS is an overlay type[36] of system that enforces movement authority and speed restrictions for ETMS-equipped trains. This system works in conjunction with the existing methods of operation, including using input from the signal system to mitigate potential human error.

At the time of this accident, ETMS was not installed at the accident site or on the locomotives. However, because both passenger and freight trains use this line, the BNSF is working on implementing ETMS on the Creston Subdivision before December 31, 2015, as mandated by the RSIA.

When installed on the Creston Subdivision, ETMS will establish signals as targets.[37] In the ETMS, a red restricting grade signal will be a target that requires restricted speed. The ETMS is designed to enforce the upper limit of restricted speed, which is 20 mph on the BNSF. As currently designed, upon reaching 3 mph over the 20-mph restriction (23 mph), a visual alarm will be displayed and an audible alarm sounded. If the engineer does not take action to reduce speed, a full service penalty brake application will be applied automatically to bring the train to a stop.

---

[35] Interoperability is needed because railroads often operate their trains on tracks of other railroads.

[36] The ETMS overlays the existing control system and enforces that system's requirements, instead of serving as a stand-alone control system that replaces the existing control system.

[37] A *target* is a location where a train-handling action must be taken (stop or reduce speed). If no action is taken, the system provides a visual and audible warning. If the engineer does not take action, the system intervenes to apply braking automatically and bring the train to a stop.

A red stop signal at CP McPherson will also be a target. The ETMS will calculate a safe braking profile for a train and automatically stop a train short of a stop signal if the engineer does not take action to slow and then stop the train. As currently designed, the rear of a standing train will not be an ETMS target.

Locomotive Alerters. BNSF road locomotives are equipped with an electronic alertness device that is called an "alerter." Alerters are designed to assist in maintaining the vigilance of the crewmembers in the locomotive cab and to apply train brakes should the device fail to detect activity. Alerters are programmed to detect engineer activity such as control lever movements, horn use, and several other parameters. When no activity is detected for a predetermined time, the alerter goes into an alarm sequence. BNSF representatives told investigators that almost all of their road locomotives are equipped with alerters and that all new locomotives are ordered with alerters.

The following is the BNSF description and instructions provided in the *Air Brake and Train Handling Rules*, effective April 7, 2010:

104.12 Electronic Alertness Device

An electronic alertness device stops the train with a service rate brake application if the engineer does not respond properly. It functions as follows:

1. The device begins functioning when locomotive brake cylinder pressure falls below 25 psi.

2. At this point, the device monitors the operator's alertness.

3. It resets when the operator changes the position of or operates one of these locomotive controls:

   - Throttle

   - Horn

   - Bell

   - Dynamic Brake, or

   - Device reset button

   - Radio transmit (on some alerter types)

4. If the device is not reset within the reset cycle (varies relative to speed):

- A warning light flashes.

- A warning horn sounds off and on for 10 seconds and then continuously for 10 seconds.

5. If the device is not reset within 20 seconds after the warning light and horn begin operating, the train brakes will automatically be applied at a service rate (Penalty Brake).

The instructions make reference to a "reset cycle," (4, above). EMD locomotives, like the one on the head end of the striking train, have a reset cycle that works as follows: alerter inactivity is about 120 seconds for speeds from 0 to 40 mph. For speeds greater than 40 mph, the following formula is used to establish the time in seconds:

$$120 \times (40/\text{Speed in mph})$$

The General Electric model specifications for the locomotives that BNSF uses have a reset cycle that works as follows: alerter inactivity is about 120 seconds for speeds from 0 to 20 mph. For speeds greater than 20 mph, the following formula is used to establish the time in seconds:

$$2,400/\text{Speed in mph}$$

Because the striking coal train's speed did not exceed 40 mph, the alerter was designed to cycle (and alarm) about every 120 seconds for more than a 30-minute period before the time of the collision. This would have included the time after the striking train had passed the red restricting grade signal that required restricted speed operation.

During the 15 minutes prior to the collision, the striking train alerter alarmed three times after periods of engineer inactivity and each time was reset using the alerter reset button after a strobe displayed for 5 seconds and an audible alarm sounded for an additional 2 to 3 seconds. The collision occurred 1 minute 53 seconds after a throttle movement, and the alerter would have been due to alarm in about 7 seconds had the collision not occurred.

1.9.9 Postaccident Actions

On April 25, 2011, the BNSF issued a safety briefing document that was used with operating employees systemwide in briefing sessions about the factual circumstances of this accident and to review and emphasize the safety-critical nature of restricted speed requirements.

The BNSF Nebraska Division implemented a pilot locomotive in-cab communication program—Reduce Exposure and Control Train (REACT)—that requires crewmembers to stay in the cab of the locomotive and to focus communications only on immediate responsibilities for safe train operation within 1 mile of the end of train authority limits. The purpose of this program is to heighten the crew's situational awareness during operations that are particularly critical for safety. Typically, the last mile before the end of train authority limits requires either operation at restricted speed or preparation for a full stop within the mile. This pilot program was introduced to labor leaders and union safety representatives with BNSF management marathons[38] given to operating employees during September 2011. In the Red Oak accident, the end of the authority limit for the striking coal train was CP McPherson, at MP 447.5. The collision occurred about MP 448.3, which is 0.8 mile from CP McPherson, thus it was within the last mile before the end of the authority limit.

---

[38] BNSF "marathons" refer to meetings in which management conducts briefings on new programs or initiatives for operating employees. The sessions usually last for 36 continuous hours or three 8-hour sessions on consecutive days and involve meeting with train crews as they come on duty.

2. Analysis

2.1 Introduction

This analysis includes discussion of the following safety issues identified in this report:

- Train crew fatigue

- Positive train control regulations and design

- Crashworthiness of modular locomotive cabs

- Survivability of electronic data

This introductory section discusses those elements of the investigation that the NTSB determined were not factors in the accident. The balance of the analysis addresses the factors that were found to have caused or contributed to the accident, or to have contributed to its severity.

The track, the signal system, the locomotives, and the rail cars were inspected and tested to the extent possible, and no defects were noted. Further, the striking coal train had received the required air brake tests and inspections before it departed Lincoln, Nebraska, before the accident, and no discrepancies were noted. Signal system data and postaccident tests and inspections indicated that the signals were functioning properly at the time of the collision.

Sight-distance observations indicated that all signals were clearly visible. A standing exemplar rear car of the struck MOW equipment train was also clearly visible.

The accident occurred in daylight with dry weather, and no visibility problems were reported.

The coroner provided specimens taken from the deceased engineer and conductor. The crew on the standing train provided required postaccident toxicological specimens. All of the test results on these specimens were negative for illegal drugs and ingested alcohol. Medical records for the deceased engineer and conductor indicated that their vision and hearing were within the limits required for their positions.

The MOW equipment train was standing at a stop signal on a track that it was authorized to occupy.

Investigators obtained telephone records of personal cellular telephones belonging to both train crews. The records indicated that no calls or texts were initiated or received during the accident trip by the crewmembers of either train.

The NTSB therefore concludes that the following were not factors in the accident: the condition of the track, railcars, or signal system; the weather; the visibility of signals; the use of cellular telephones by crewmembers; the vision and hearing of the crew; illegal drug or alcohol use, the actions of the train dispatcher and the crew of the MOW equipment train; or the mechanical condition of the locomotives of the striking coal train.

2.2   Striking Train Crew Performance

After passing the red restricting grade signal, the crew of the striking train had ample opportunity to slow and stop their train to avoid a collision. However, neither crewmember applied the train's brakes to slow or stop the train despite the fact that the standing train ahead was visible for 43 seconds leading up to impact. During nearly 2 minutes before it struck the standing train, the train travelled nearly 3,344 feet. During this time, the striking coal train's speed increased because of the descending grade, and event recorder data indicate that no control inputs were made. Investigators examined the crew's work schedule factors, medical histories, and activities captured by the event recorder to better understand why the crewmembers took no action to stop the coal train before impact.

2.2.1 Work Schedule Factors

During the week leading up to the accident, the engineer worked both day and night schedules. On the day of the accident, the engineer went on duty at 2:31 a.m. The day before, he was on duty from 4:30 a.m. to 2:30 p.m. He had not been called for duty on the 2 previous days. Although investigators were unable to determine his off-duty activities and rest periods during those days, it is likely that he was awake during the day and slept at night. During the 3 days immediately prior to that, he was on duty during the daytime for engineer recertification and official union activities. It is thus likely that for several days leading up to the day before the accident, the engineer was awake during the daytime hours and slept at night. Adjusting to different sleep schedules can take several days, depending on the difference between the previous and the current schedule.[39] During this time, people often suffer from sleep disruption while trying to sleep during a different time of day, leading to a sleep-deprived state. On the day of the accident, the engineer probably was still adjusting to a nighttime work schedule after spending several days sleeping at night. Consequently, he may have experienced short-term sleep loss resulting in acute fatigue.

The conductor had worked a nighttime work schedule over the 4 days leading up to the accident. Studies have found that the sleep quality of night shift workers, and

---

[39] Information from the National Institutes of Health.

consequently their alertness levels, is generally inferior to those of people who work a normal (daytime) schedule.[40] Thus the conductor's alertness level also may have been affected by her recent nighttime work schedule.

The accident occurred at 6:55 a.m., just after sunrise, at a time of day when the crew may have been experiencing reduced alertness as a result of their circadian rhythms. Circadian rhythms are physical, mental, and behavioral changes that follow a roughly 24-hour cycle, responding primarily to light and darkness. They influence sleep-wake cycles, hormone release, body temperature, and other important bodily functions. Circadian rhythms and alertness levels are typically at their lowest between 3:00 a.m. and 5:00 a.m. and continue to rise for several hours after this. During these low periods, physiological and mental functioning are reduced and human performance is most degraded. Although the accident occurred about 2 hours after what is typically the lowest point in circadian rhythms, the crew were still at a relatively low point in this cycle and may have continued to be less alert and experiencing fatigue.

Both the conductor and the engineer had worked irregular schedules for several weeks leading up to the accident. During this time, work start times often varied significantly from day to day for both crewmembers. Over the last month before the accident, the conductor, who had been on duty for 12 of the last 13 days before the accident, had start times that varied on consecutive days so that her start time was between 1 and 8 hours earlier or later than her start time on the previous day. For instance, on April 7, 8, and 9, her work start times were 2:16 p.m., 10:15 p.m., and 4:40 p.m., respectively. Similarly, for the engineer, over the last month his work start times often varied by several hours on consecutive days. For example, on April 8, 9, and 10, his shift start times were 12:40 a.m., 2:00 p.m., and 9:21 a.m., respectively. Changing work start and end times can make achieving adequate sleep more difficult. That is, irregular work schedules tend to disrupt a person's normal circadian rhythms and sleep patterns, which in turn can lead to chronic fatigue. Moreover, studies of train accidents have shown that very irregular schedules contributed to the accidents by producing sleep loss and fatigue.[41] Therefore, the NTSB concludes that the striking coal train conductor's and the engineer's irregular work schedules contributed to their being fatigued on the morning of the collision.

On the day before the accident, the crew operated their train from 4:30 a.m. to 2:30 p.m. and spent the night in a nearby hotel. After crews arrive at their terminals, sometimes they can get a reasonable estimate of their next on-duty time and attempt to adjust their sleep schedules to get sufficient sleep before their departure. For the striking coal train engineer in particular, who in the last few days was keeping a daytime schedule, getting adequate sleep before the start of his next shift would have been difficult. That is, rather than going to bed at nighttime, he would have to go to bed in the

---

[40] G. Richardson and H. Malin, "Circadian Rhythm Sleep Disorders: Pathophysiology and Treatment," *Journal of Clinical Neurophysiology*, vol. 13, no. 1, January (1996), pp. 17–31.

[41] W. Maynard and G. Brogmus, "Shiftwork, work scheduling and safety: How much is too much," 10th Annual Applied Ergonomics Conference (2007).

afternoon in order to receive sufficient sleep. This phase advance[42] of several hours and would have resulted in significant sleep latency[43] and shortened total sleep time.[44] Moreover, because of the significant variability in their work schedules that had occurred often during the last month, the need of both crewmembers to adjust to significant phase advances may have resulted in a cumulative sleep debt.

2.2.2 Medical Factors

Although the conductor had never undergone a sleep study, she had several risk factors for obstructive sleep apnea (OSA), including a BMI[45] of 37.5, a history of hypertension, and long periods of sitting.[46] OSA is a disorder characterized by repeated episodes of upper airway obstruction that results in recurrent arousals during sleep. The "apnea" in OSA refers to a cessation of airflow that lasts at least 10 seconds. The cessation of airflow occurs when the muscles in the back of the throat fail to keep the airway open, despite efforts to breathe. Several studies have shown an association between BMI and the risk of OSA.[47] Significant OSA is present in 40 percent of obese people.[48] The conductor's BMI placed her within this risk group. The conductor was also being treated for high blood pressure with two prescription medications, but she still was hypertensive. OSA is associated with high blood pressure.[49] Since people with sleep apnea tend to be sleep deprived, they often suffer from sleepiness and a wide range of other symptoms such as difficulty concentrating, depression, learning and memory difficulties, and falling asleep while at work, on the phone, or driving. Left untreated,

---

[42] A *phase advance* is a backward shift in the 24-hour sleep-wake cycle. For example, shifting from an 11:00 p.m. to 7:00 a.m. sleep phase to an 8:00 p.m. to 4:00 a.m. sleep phase.

[43] *Sleep latency* is the amount of time it takes to fall asleep after the lights have been turned off.

[44] (a) S. Folkard and J. Barton, "Does the 'Forbidden Zone' for Sleep Onset Influence Morning Shift Sleep Duration?," *Ergonomics*, vol. 36, no. 1–3 (January 1993), pp. 85–91. (b) T. Monk and others, "Inducing Jet-Lag in Older People: Directional Asymmetry," *Journal of Sleep Research*, vol. 9 (2000), pp. 101–116. (c) R. Manfredini and others, "Circadian Rhythms, Athletic Performance, and Jet Lag," *British Journal of Sports Medicine*, vol. 32 (1998), pp. 101–106.

[45] Obesity is defined as a BMI of 30 and above, according to the National Institutes of Health. People who fall into the BMI range of 25 to 34.9 and have a waist size of over 40 inches for men and 35 inches for women are considered to be at especially high risk for health problems.

[46] A joint task force of the American College of Chest Physicians, American College of Occupational and Environmental Medicine, and the National Sleep Foundation developed screening recommendations for drivers with possible OSA. Five major categories were identified. Additional evaluation was recommended for commercial drivers who had two or more of the following: A BMI $\geq$ 35; a neck circumference greater than 17 inches for men and 16 inches for women; and hypertension (new, uncontrolled, or unable to control with less than two medications).

[47] T. Young, P.E. Peppard, and S. Taheri, "Excess weight and sleep-disordered breathing," *Journal of Applied Physiology,* 99(4), Oct. (2005), pp. 1592–9 contains a list of studies that show the association between BMI and OSA risk.

[48] A.N. Vgontzas and others, "Sleep apnea and sleep disruption in obese patients," *Archives of Internal Medicine,* vol. 154, no. 15, Aug 8 (1994), pp. 1705–11.

[49] F.J. Nieto and others, "Association of Sleep-Disordered Breathing, Sleep Apnea, and Hypertension in a Large Community-Based Study," *Journal of the American Medical Association*, vol. 283, no. 14 (2000), pp. 1829–1836.

OSA can result in other clinical consequences including disturbed sleep, excessive sleepiness, high blood pressure, heart attack, congestive heart failure, cardiac arrhythmia, stroke, or depression.[50] The conductor was treated for restless legs syndrome (a movement disorder that typically interferes with sleep) with ropinirole. Ropinirole is a medication for Parkinson's disease that sometimes results in sleepiness in Parkinson's patients. Additionally, she had been prescribed a medication for insomnia. Thus, it appears that she was not sleeping well, which may have resulted in her being fatigued. The conductor also had been prescribed an antidepressant medication. Lack of sleep has been linked to depression.[51]

The engineer had never undergone a sleep study, although he, too, had several risk factors associated with OSA: a BMI of 35.7; his gender (men are twice as likely as women to have sleep apnea); and job duties that required prolonged sitting. In addition, he had type 2 diabetes. Recent reports have indicated that the majority of patients with type 2 diabetes also have OSA.[52]

The NTSB concludes that based on their medical histories, both crewmembers on the striking coal train were at high risk for sleep disorders and fatigue.

2.2.3 Crew Actions Leading up to Collision

Based on the indication of the clearly visible red (restricting) signal located almost 2 miles before the point of collision, the crew was required to operate their train at restricted speed—a speed that allowed the train to be stopped within one-half the range of vision short of another train, not to exceed 20 mph. Operating at restricted speed, they should have reduced speed and come to a stop short of the standing train. The crew, however, made no attempt to slow or stop the train during the last 1 minute 53 seconds before impact. As the striking train continued to travel around a curve, the operating crew would have been able to see the clearly visible car at the rear of the MOW train from more than 1/4 mile away (about 46 seconds before impact). This provided adequate time for them to apply emergency brakes that may have stopped, or at least slowed, their train before impact. However, despite having enough time to take action, the crew made no attempt to apply the brakes or stop their train to avoid the collision.

During the last 15 minutes of the trip and while the striking train was approaching the standing MOW equipment train, the engineer reset the alerter by pressing the reset button three times after prompting by a lengthy strobe and audible alarm sequence.[53]

---

[50] Information from the National Sleep Foundation.

[51] N. Tsuno, A. Bessett, and K. Ritchie, "Sleep and depression," *Journal of Clinical Psychiatry*, vol. 66, no. 10 (2005), pp. 1254–1269.

[52] E. Tasali, B. Mokhlesi, and E. Van Cauter, "Obstructive sleep apnea and type 2 diabetes: interacting epidemics," *Ches*, vol. 133, no. 2, Feb. (2008), pp. 496–506.

[53] When the alerter system does not detect engineer activity, it will alarm (strobe light followed by horn). The alarm can be silenced by moving a control lever or by pressing the reset button.

These resets were initiated only after 5 seconds of flashing strobe and an additional 2 to 3 seconds of an increasingly louder audible alarm. The reset button requires less attentiveness than actually manipulating the controls of the engine.

The operational documents issued to the crew of the striking coal train were reviewed. There were no speed restrictions, track bulletins, or other advisories in effect that would have required the crew's attention as their train crested the grade and approached the standing train. However, since the last signal required the striking coal train to operate at restricted speed, the 25-mph speed restriction did not apply to this train. Investigators could not identify any job-related activity that would have distracted the crew from focusing on operating the train in accordance with the restricting signal indication and preparing to stop short of a standing train ahead.

Investigators considered the possibility that both the engineer and the conductor were impaired by fatigue at the time of the accident. In general, fatigue results in a reduction in alertness, longer reaction times, memory problems, poorer psychometric coordination, and less efficient information processing.[54] Fatigue also could lead to the onset of an episode of microsleep, in which a person enters a sleeping period that lasts from a few seconds to as long as half a minute, becomes unresponsive, and fails to respond to outside information.[55] However, given the crew's failure to attempt to slow or stop the train for nearly 2 minutes despite explicit warnings, it is likely that the crew was impaired by more than temporary fatigue-related loss of focus or an episode of microsleep. The NTSB concludes that based on the conductor's and the engineer's irregular work schedules, their medical histories, and their lack of action before the collision, both crewmembers on the striking coal train had fallen asleep due to fatigue.

2.3 Fatigue

2.3.1 Fatigue Education at BNSF

In 2004, the BNSF developed a computer (and later, a web-based) fatigue training program, "The Science of Sleep and Fatigue," that was available to all BNSF employees.[56] This training could be taken at a BNSF facility or at the employee's home. There are currently no Federal regulations requiring railroads to provide fatigue educational programs, nor does the BNSF require its employees to take this training. At the time of the accident, 239 BNSF employees, or about 1 percent,[57] had voluntarily

---

[54] I.D. Brown, "Driver fatigue," *Ergonomics*, vol. 36 (1994), pp. 298–314.

[55] M.R. Rosekind and others, "Alertness Management in Long-Haul Flight Operations," in *Proceedings of the 39th Annual Corporate Aviation Safety Seminar* (St. Louis, Missouri: Flight Safety Foundation, 1994), pp. 167–178.

[56] The BNSF stated that a significant portion of the information in this training program was originally developed by NASA for the aviation industry and later adapted to other safety-sensitive industries, including the railroad industry.

[57] The fatigue training program is designed for the people (about 20,000) who work in the BNSF transportation department.

completed the fatigue training program. Neither the conductor nor the engineer of the coal train had taken this training.

Investigators reviewed the BNSF training program and believe that it presents valuable and scientifically based information that would benefit railroad employees operating in safety-critical positions. The information presented in the BNSF's fatigue training program encourages people who are at risk of suffering from OSA or other sleep disorders to consult a physician. As stated previously, neither the engineer nor the conductor of the striking train had undergone a sleep study, although both were at risk for sleep apnea.

The NTSB has a long history of making recommendations in all modes of transportation to reduce the likelihood of fatigue-related accidents. In the railroad industry, the scope of the NTSB's recommendations have included requiring railroads to use scientifically based principles when assigning work schedules; requiring railroads to design work schedules to minimize irregular and unpredictable work-rest cycles; establishing requirements that limit train crewmember limbo time; developing a standard medical form that includes questions about sleep problems; requiring serious and potentially impairing medical conditions to be reported to and evaluated by the carrier; and requiring railroads to develop fatigue awareness training.

The NTSB concludes that had the two crewmembers on the striking coal train completed the BNSF's fatigue training program, they would have had the opportunity to learn that they were at risk for sleep disorders, particularly obstructive sleep apnea, and the computer-based training program would have displayed a message advising them to consult with a physician. Therefore, the NTSB recommends that the BNSF require all employees and managers who perform or supervise safety-critical tasks to complete fatigue training on an annual basis and document when they have received this training.

2.3.2 Fatigue Management and Rail Safety Improvement Act of 2008

Congress enacted the Rail Safety Improvement Act of 2008 (RSIA) following the September 12, 2008, head-on collision between a passenger train and a freight train in Chatsworth, California.[58] The RSIA requires the Secretary of Transportation to require that most passenger and freight railroads develop fatigue management plans. The RSIA gives railroads 4 years after enactment of the law in which to develop these plans, which must include methods to manage and reduce fatigue experienced by railroad employees in safety-related positions and to reduce the likelihood of accidents, incidents, injuries, and fatalities caused by fatigue. There are several elements to the RSIA's fatigue

---

[58] *Collision of Metrolink Train 111 With Union Pacific Train LOF65–12, Chatsworth, California, September 12, 2008,* Railroad Accident Report NTSB/RAR-10/01 (Washington, D.C.: National Transportation Safety Board, 2010). <http://www.ntsb.gov>

management plan requirements, many of which are relevant to this accident.[59] Three of these elements are listed here and discussed below:

> Employee education and training on the physiological and human factors that affect fatigue, as well as strategies to reduce or mitigate the effects of fatigue, based on the most current scientific and medical research and literature.

> Opportunities for identification, diagnosis, and treatment of any medical condition that may affect alertness or fatigue, including sleep disorders.

> Scheduling practices for employees, including innovative scheduling practices, on-duty call practices, work and rest cycles, increased consecutive days off for employees, changes in shift patterns, appropriate scheduling practices for varying types of work, and other aspects of employee scheduling that would reduce employee fatigue and cumulative sleep loss.

In a December 19, 2011, letter, the FRA advised the NTSB that it is "currently in the process of drafting guidance for railroads to develop Fatigue Management Plans as part of a larger railroad risk reduction program." The guidance is expected to be issued in early 2013. The FRA also has recently formed an RSAC working group to provide advice on developing fatigue management plans.

Employee Education and Training on Fatigue. The NTSB believes that fatigue education and training should be required on a recurring basis for all railroad employees operating in safety-critical functions. The NTSB previously has recommended, and continues to strongly support, fatigue education and training for railroad employees. An RSAC working group on passenger hours of service, formed as a result of the RSIA, recommended that employees be required to take training on fatigue every 3 years. While the BNSF and many other railroads have developed fatigue training programs, most do not require their employees to take this type of training. An effective and comprehensive fatigue training program should cover the broad range of causation factors, countermeasures, and mitigation strategies; personal strategies for maintaining alertness (such as strategic napping); and medically based sleep disorders such as OSA that can affect a crewmember's ability to receive adequate sleep.

The FRA and the Volpe National Transportation Systems Center are currently collaborating to develop a fatigue website for freight and passenger train crews. The website, which is expected to be launched in May 2012, is designed to appeal to a typical train operating employee—male, middle-aged, possibly overweight, who remains seated for long hours and often works unpredictable schedules. The website will offer text and video links to discussions of topics related to sleep and fatigue including scientific information about fatigue; practical strategies to deal with fatigue; and information on sleep disorders, such as OSA, insomnia, and restless legs syndrome. Railroads providing

---

[59] Title 49 *United States Code* (U.S.C.), chapter 201, subchapter II, section 20156. "Railroad safety risk reduction program."

passenger service are required by 49 CFR Part 228 to provide train operating employees with initial and refresher fatigue awareness training. The FRA advised the NTSB that fatigue awareness training requirements for freight operations will be discussed by the RSAC working group addressing fatigue management plans.

Identification, Diagnosis, and Treatment of Medical Conditions Affecting Fatigue. Based in large part on the NTSB recommendations made after the 2001 train collision in Clarkston, Michigan,[60] the FRA formed an RSAC working group on medical standards for safety-critical personnel. The NTSB safety recommendations from the Clarkston accident investigation are the following:

To Canadian National Railway:

> Require all your employees in safety-sensitive positions to take fatigue awareness training and document when employees have received this training. (R-02-23)

To the FRA:

> Develop a standard medical examination form that includes questions regarding sleep problems and require that the form be used, pursuant to 49 CFR Part 240, to determine the medical fitness of locomotive engineers; the form should also be available for use to determine the medical fitness of other employees in safety-sensitive positions. (R-02-24)

> Require that any medical condition that could incapacitate, or seriously impair the performance of, an employee in a safety-sensitive position be reported to the railroad in a timely manner. (R-02-25)

> Require that, when a railroad becomes aware that an employee in a safety-sensitive position has a potentially incapacitating or performance-impairing medical condition, the railroad prohibit that employee from performing any safety-sensitive duties until the railroad's designated physician determines that the employee can continue to work safely in a safety-sensitive position. (R-02-26)

The first working group meeting was held on December 12–13, 2006, 5 1/2 years ago. The purpose of the working group was to enhance the safety of railroad employees and the public by establishing standards and procedures for determining the medical fitness for duty of personnel engaged in safety-critical functions. A physicians' task force, established by the working group, has been working since May 2007 on developing medical guidelines that will be used to provide consistent criteria for determining the medical fitness for duty of those in safety-critical positions. The task force has been compiling a list of medical conditions that can cause sudden incapacitation

---

[60] *Collision of Two Canadian National/Illinois Central Railway Trains Near Clarkston, Michigan, November 15, 2001*, Railroad Accident Report NTSB/RAR-02/04 (Washington, D.C.: National Transportation Safety Board, 2002). <http://www.ntsb.gov>

and serious impairments of hearing and vision, determining the elements to be included in a health history form that covered employees will complete, and determining the medical criteria (standards) that a covered employee must meet to be certified. A draft Notice of Proposed Rulemaking (NPRM) was developed by the FRA and presented to the working group. The original target date for publishing the NPRM was December 2009. This NPRM was never published. It is disturbing that such an important railroad safety issue is taking this long to address.

The FRA recently has advised the NTSB that a regulation to address medical fitness for duty of railroad safety critical personnel is no longer being considered because of the high cost to railroads. Instead, the FRA indicated that it will produce nonmandatory recommendations for the industry. The RSAC working group will be reconvened at some future date to finalize these recommendations. Obstructive sleep apnea will be addressed separately as part of the fatigue management regulation currently in development. The NTSB is disappointed that the FRA will not promulgate a requirement to ensure that operating employees in safety-sensitive positions are medically fit for duty. The NTSB concludes that had the requirements described in Safety Recommendations R-02-24, -25, and -26 been in place, this crew would likely have been identified as at high risk for sleep disorders, which may have led to appropriate medical intervention. Therefore, the NTSB recommends that the FRA require railroads to medically screen employees in safety-sensitive positions for sleep apnea and other sleep disorders. Additionally, the NTSB recommends that the BNSF medically screen employees in safety-sensitive positions for sleep apnea and other sleep disorders. The NTSB also reiterates Safety Recommendations R-02-24, -25, and -26 to the FRA and hopes that the FRA will take prompt action.

Scheduling Practices for Employees. The NTSB previously has recommended incorporating scientifically based principles when creating work schedules. The NTSB is cognizant of several biomathematical models of fatigue and performance either currently used or proposed for use in various modes of transportation, including aviation and railroads, to help predict the risk of incidents caused by crewmember fatigue based on work schedules and opportunities to sleep. Biomathematical models of fatigue attempt to predict the effects of various work patterns on job performance. They also consider scientific input about the relationship among working hours, sleep, and employee performance. The FRA is advocating the use by commuter and passenger railroads of models that the FRA indicated have been validated and calibrated, such as the Fatigue Avoidance Scheduling Tool and the Fatigue Audit InterDyne Model.[61] The RSIA does not specify the role of the FRA in evaluating the railroad industry's use of biomathematical models of fatigue and performance.

The NTSB is aware, however, of some general limitations regarding the use of these models. For instance, in general, biomathematical models have been calibrated to represent a population average rather than real-time fatigue levels of a specific

---

[61] The FRA has conducted an evaluation of six of the most recognized alertness models and is currently funding a project to develop a method of correlating the results among models.

individual.[62] It is unclear how individual differences (such as age, sex, and operating experience) may affect the output of these models. Additionally, biomathematical fatigue models predict risk factors for an average healthy person; thus, the output may not accurately predict the risks to a crewmember who may have medical conditions or otherwise not be fully fit for duty. The NTSB further recognizes that biomathematical models may not consider all factors affecting fatigue such as workload (mental or physical, high or low cognitive demand), the operating environment (including lighting, temperature, and noise level), and pharmacological agents, for example, caffeine and changes in adrenaline levels due to stressors. Other factors that may not be represented in biomathematical models include stressors in the workplace (that is, time pressure, social friction) and aspects of the work (such as monotony and repetitive motion).[63] Studies have pointed out the need for additional research to determine whether one or more of these work-related factors are important alone or in interaction with sleep/wake cycles and circadian dynamics, especially for risk-focused models.[64] The NTSB notes that several studies have concluded that fatigue model predictions cannot be the sole means upon which fatigue risk management operational decisions are made.[65] The NTSB concludes that because biomathematical models of fatigue are relatively new to the railroad industry, the use of this technology should be evaluated for its effectiveness within the context of railroads' fatigue management plans through independent scientific peer review. Therefore, the NTSB recommends that the FRA establish an ongoing program to monitor, evaluate, report on, and continuously improve fatigue management systems implemented by operating railroads to identify, mitigate, and continuously reduce fatigue-related risks for personnel performing safety-critical tasks, with particular emphasis on biomathematical models of fatigue.

2.3.3 Locomotive Alerters

Locomotive alerter technology was developed to provide a countermeasure to operator fatigue and incapacity.[66] Alerters in use on North American railroads have evolved from a "deadman pedal"[67] to the type of activity-based alerter installed on the striking coal train locomotive. The current type of alerter commonly in use on North American railroads detects engineer activity through control handle movements. When activity is not detected for a predetermined time interval, an alarm is activated that

---

[62] *Biomathematical Fatigue Modeling in Civil Aviation Fatigue Risk Management,* Australian Government Civil Aviation Safety Authority Human Factors Section, March 2010.

[63] D. Dinges, "Critical Research Issues in Development of Biomathematical Models of Fatigue and Performance," *Aviation, Space, and Environmental Medicine,* vol. 75, no. 3, section II, March (2004).

[64] D. Dinges references relevant studies.

[65] D. Dinges references relevant studies.

[66] C.M. Oman and A.M. Liu, *Locomotive In-Cab Alerter Technology Assessment,* Man Vehicle Laboratory Report #07.30 (Cambridge, MA: Massachusetts Institute of Technology, 2007) provides a good historical overview.

[67] A *deadman pedal* is a device that was used on some early diesel and electric locomotives. The engineer was required to keep the pedal depressed to keep the locomotive moving. If the pedal was released while the locomotive was in motion, braking was automatically activated.

can be reset by manipulating a reset button or moving a control handle. The alerter time interval is typically programmed to be speed dependent, with the alerter set to alarm at a shorter time interval at higher speeds.

Previous Alerter Recommendations. The NTSB has investigated dozens of railroad accidents over the decades in which crew alertness was a causal factor, and it has repeatedly examined the role of locomotive alerter technology.

In its investigation of the collision of two Consolidated Rail Corporation (Conrail) freight trains in 1988,[68] the NTSB found that the accident was caused by the sleep-deprived condition of the crew and their consequent failure to comply with a signal. After examining the role of alerters in that accident, the NTSB concluded that had the locomotive of the striking train "been equipped with a state-of-the-art alertness device, the train would have been stopped and the collision would have been avoided."

In the collision of two Norfolk Southern Railway freight trains at Sugar Valley, Georgia,[69] on August 9, 1990, the crew of one of the trains failed to stop at a signal. The NTSB concluded that the engineer of that train was probably experiencing an episode of microsleep or was distracted. Postaccident testing indicated that as the train approached the stop signal, the alerter would have begun an alarm cycle. The NTSB concluded that the engineer "could have cancelled the alerter system while he was asleep by a simple reflex action that he performed without conscious thought." As a result of the investigation, the NTSB made the following recommendation to the FRA:

> In conjunction with the study of fatigue of train crewmembers, explore the parameters of an optimum alerter system for locomotives. (R-91-26)

The FRA responded to this recommendation on June 28, 1993, stating that it had "awarded two contracts to develop proposals to modify the existing alerter systems so that they cannot be reset by reflex action." In a follow-up letter dated August 12, 1997, the FRA told the NTSB that although a proposal for a prototype had been developed, the contractor had told the FRA that it "could not see a market for the device large enough to justify its further development." The FRA told the NTSB that it believed that the lack of a market was a result of the FRA's own "announced determination" to support positive train separation technology. As a result, the NTSB classified Safety Recommendation R-91-26 "Closed—Unacceptable Action" on November 4, 1997.

---

[68] *Head-end Collision of Consolidated Rail Corporation Freight Trains UBT-506 and TV-61 Near Thompsontown, Pennsylvania, January 14, 1988*, Railroad Accident Report NTSB/RAR-89/02 (Washington, D.C.: National Transportation Safety Board, 1989). <http://www.ntsb.gov>

[69] *Collision and Derailment of Norfolk Southern Train 188 with Norfolk Southern Train G-38 at Sugar Valley, Georgia, August 9, 1990*, Railroad Accident Report NTSB/RAR-91/02 (Washington, D.C.: National Transportation Safety Board, 1991). <http://www.ntsb.gov>

As a result of an investigation into a July 2, 1997, sideswipe collision between two Union Pacific Railroad (UP) freight trains in Delia, Kansas,[70] the NTSB concluded that "had the striking locomotive been equipped with an alerter, it may have helped the engineer stay awake while his train traveled through the siding." As a result of its investigation, the NTSB made the following recommendation to the FRA:

> Revise the Federal regulations to require that all locomotives operating on lines that do not have a positive train separation system be equipped with a cognitive alerter system that cannot be reset by reflex action. (R-99-53)[71]

In an April 28, 2000, letter, the FRA told the NTSB that it had issued regulations requiring that "each passenger train not equipped with a positive train separation system be equipped with a working dead man or alerter." Although this was an important safety improvement, the FRA's regulations neglected to address the critical components of Safety Recommendation R-99-53. The FRA's regulations applied only to passenger trains, and they did not require the installation of cognitive alerters. On September 25, 2000, the NTSB responded that it was disappointed that the FRA's new safety standards applied only to passenger locomotives and not to freight locomotives. The NTSB classified Safety Recommendation R-99-53 "Closed—Reconsidered" on August 6, 2002, after concluding that the type of cognitive alerter envisioned at the time the recommendation was issued did not exist.

As a result of its investigation of the Delia accident, the NTSB also recommended that the UP

> Install a cognitive alerter system that cannot be reset by reflex action on all locomotives that operate on lines that do not have a positive train separation system. (R-99-59)

In a response dated October 31, 2000, the UP told the NTSB that the alerters it was installing on some existing locomotives and on new locomotives were "cognitive ... [and] considered to be state-of-the-art in the industry." The UP letter added that although "the level of cognition is not optimal, there are no more sophisticated alerters available in the market today." Based on the UP's response, the NTSB classified Safety Recommendation R-99-59 "Closed—Acceptable Alternate Action" on April 24, 2001.

The most recent NTSB recommendations relating to locomotive alerters were made as a result of an investigation into a head-on collision between two freight trains

---

[70] *Collision Between Union Pacific Freight Trains MKSNP-01 and ZSEME-29 near Delia, Kansas, July 2, 1997*, Railroad Accident Report NTSB/RAR-99/04 (Washington, D.C.: National Transportation Safety Board, 1999). <http://www.ntsb.gov>

[71] Currently, all alerters are reset by reflex action or manipulation of the train controls. In 1999, a cognitive alerter was considered to be an alerter that would have required more than a simple reflex action from the crew.

near Anding, Mississippi.[72] In that accident, the northbound train overran a stop signal at high speed, likely as a result of fatigue-related inattention. The resulting head-on collision claimed the lives of all crewmembers on both trains. The controlling locomotive on the overrunning train was not equipped with an alerter. The NTSB noted that

> There was a 4-minute time period after passing the approach signal during which the alerter would have activated four to five times. It seems unlikely that the engineer could have reset the alerter multiple times by reflex action without any increase in his awareness. Therefore, an alerter likely would have detected the lack of activity on the part of the engineer and sounded an alarm that could have alerted one or both crewmembers.

Based on the Anding collision investigation, the NTSB made recommendations on alerters to the FRA and to all Class I railroads.

To the FRA:

> Require railroads to ensure that the lead locomotives used to operate trains on tracks not equipped with a positive train control system are equipped with an alerter. (R-07-1)

In an NPRM published in the *Federal Register* on January 12, 2011,[73] the FRA provided notice of its intent to revise existing railroad locomotive safety standards, including regulations on alerters. The NPRM section on alerters proposes to require locomotives that operate over 25 mph to be equipped with an alerter meeting specified performance standards. One of the performance standards relates to the requirement that the alerter will reset in response to at least three different commands. The FRA describes the intent of the reset requirements as follows:

> Utilizing several different reset options for the warning timing cycle increases the effectiveness of the alerter, as it would require differentiated cognitive actions by the operator. This will help prevent the operator from repeating the same reset many times as a reflex, without having full awareness of the action.

The NPRM public comment period closed on March 14, 2011. On April 9, 2012, the FRA published a final rule in the *Federal Register*[74] revising 49 CFR 229.140, adding the requirement for alerters on freight trains to the locomotive safety standards. The new regulation requires that a locomotive placed in service on or after June 10, 2013, be equipped with a functioning alerter when used as a controlling locomotive and if operated in excess of 25 mph. Petitions for reconsideration must be received on or before

---

[72] *Collision of Two CN Freight Trains, Anding, Mississippi, July 10, 2005*, Railroad Accident Report NTSB/RAR-07/01 (Washington, D.C.: National Transportation Safety Board, 2007). <http://www.ntsb.gov>

[73] 76 *Federal Register* (January 12, 2011), pp. 2400–2238.

[74] 77 *Federal Register* (April 9, 2012), pp. 21312–21357.

June 8, 2012. As with all of the FRA's regulatory requirements, the requirements related to alerters are minimum Federal safety requirements that do not prohibit railroads from doing more to improve railroad safety. Based on industry meetings, the NTSB understands that the industry is considering establishing industry requirements that would be more restrictive than the Federal requirements. The NTSB fully supports such an effort by the industry. Based on the intent of the requirements of the locomotive safety standards, accordingly, Safety Recommendation R-07-1 is classified "Closed—Acceptable Action."

To All Class I Railroads:

> Ensure that alerters are installed on all your lead locomotives used to operate trains on tracks not equipped with a positive train control system. (R-07-8)

This recommendation has been closed for five of the seven Class I railroad recipients. Table 3 shows all the recipients of the recommendation, the current classification of the recommendation, and the date the recommendation was closed, if applicable.

Table 3. Safety Recommendation R-07-8 Status.

Recipient/Class I Railroad	Current Classification	Date Closed
BNSF	Closed—Reconsidered	October 5, 2007
Canadian National Railway Company	Closed—Acceptable Action	June 22, 2011
Canadian Pacific Railway	Open—Acceptable Response	N/A
CSX Transportation	Closed—Acceptable Action	May 11, 2010
Kansas City Southern Railway Company	Open—Await Response	N/A
Norfolk Southern Corporation	Closed—Reconsidered	February 29, 2008
Union Pacific Railroad	Closed—Reconsidered	August 19, 2010

The Kansas City Southern Railway Company's entire road locomotive fleet is equipped with alerters. Therefore, this recommendation to Kansas City Southern Railway Company is classified "Closed—Acceptable Action." The Canadian Pacific Railway's entire main line fleet of 6-axle locomotives is equipped with alerters. Some 4-axle locomotives used in yard service and operating in road switcher service on the Canadian Pacific Railway's U.S. lines are not equipped with alerters. Also, all new 4-axle locomotives purchased are equipped with alerters including the replacements for the 4-axle fleet. The recommendation to the Canadian Pacific Railway remains "Open—Acceptable Response."

Although the NTSB considers a safety-redundant PTC system (not alerters) to be the preferred method for preventing collisions, it recognizes that there will be tracks that are not PTC equipped on many miles of the U.S. railroad network. Even had PTC been in place at the location of the Red Oak accident, the current PTC designs will not always prevent restricted-speed collisions. The circumstances of this accident demonstrate that collisions in the 20 mph range can have catastrophic consequences. Additionally, freight trains carrying hazardous materials can have a devastating effect on communities should the materials be released as a result of an accident, even at restricted speeds. Alerters will remain an important safety device that can prevent unsafe train operation after an engineer becomes unresponsive for a prolonged period of time.

Alerters and the Red Oak Collision. In the Red Oak accident, since train speed before the collision was less than 40 mph for more than 20 minutes, the alerter alarmed at about 2-minute intervals if no engineer activity was detected. The Red Oak collision occurred at a time when restricted speed was required. Safe operation at restricted speed requires maximum crew vigilance and alertness. The alerter installed on the striking train in the Red Oak accident was programmed to alarm after about 2 minutes with no activity detected. At higher speeds, it was programmed to have a shorter alarm cycle.

Railroad restricted speed is not a numerical value. The restricted speed rule on most railroads starts with the phrase, "... movement must be made at a speed that allows stopping within half the range of vision short of ...." This phrase is followed by a list of potential hazards such as train, engine, and railroad car. To ensure the safe operation of following trains, this performance portion of the restricted speed rule must be stressed rather than the importance of any maximum speed limit (20 mph on the BNSF). Several recent rear-end collisions of railroad trains in which crewmembers failed to operate their trains at the required restricted speed are discussed in this report in section 2.4.1.

The operation of the striking coal train in the vicinity of the grade signal at a speed of 11 to 12 mph is more consistent with the operational intent of restricted speed (stopping in one-half the range of vision). Visibility was good, and the train brakes were functioning properly. Had this speed been maintained and had the crew been alert to the clearly visible standing MOW equipment train, they could easily have stopped short and prevented the accident. Therefore, the NTSB concludes that had the crew of the striking coal train been alert and operated their train in accordance with restricted speed requirements, the collision would have been prevented.

Previously, the NTSB has noted that alerter reset and even minor locomotive control adjustments can occur during microsleep. The following excerpt from the NTSB's report on the collision of a Union Pacific freight train with a BNSF freight train at Macdona, Texas,[75] explains this phenomenon.

---

[75] *Collision of Union Pacific Railroad Train MHOTU-23 With BNSF Railway Company Train MEAP-TUL-126-D With Subsequent Derailment and Hazardous Materials Release, Macdona, Texas, June 28, 2004*, Railroad Accident Report NTSB/RAR-06/03 (Washington, D.C.: National Transportation Safety Board, 2006). <http://www.ntsb.gov>

That the [Macdona] engineer could have remained sufficiently alert to make train control inputs and yet be unable to respond to vitally important signal indications may be explained by the fact that making such inputs and manipulating the alerter are highly practiced, nearly reflexive, motor responses that require only lower level cognitive effort. During the engineer's transition from wakefulness into the normal perceptual disengagement of unintended sleep, his capacity for information processing would have been severely compromised. Thus, he could have been able to continue the reflexive control activities while being unable to perform the higher level cognitive tasks of extrapolating information from the signal indications.

In the Red Oak collision, the last throttle change occurred 1 minute 53 seconds before impact. After that throttle change, the train travelled 3,344 feet and speed increased from 18 to 23 mph. The rear car of the standing train was visible for 1,364 feet. During the last 1,364 feet of travel, there was no recorded activity by the engineer and the train speed increased from 20 to 23 mph. The rear of the standing train would have been visible to the crew of the striking train for about 43 seconds. The event recorder indicated that neither the engineer nor the conductor applied the brakes before impact. The alerter had sounded three times in a period of 12 minutes, and the engineer had silenced (reset) the alerter after each alarm, but the alerter was not effective in that the engineer did not respond by controlling train speed and stopping the train before the collision. The emergency brakes applied only as a result of collision damage to the airbrake system.

The FRA's requirement that alerters be installed on passenger trains and the NPRM to require alerters on freight trains operating above 25 mph will have positive safety benefits. However, it is appropriate to revisit the need for technology that is more effective, particularly during safety-critical operations such as restricted speed. PTC as currently designed will allow restricted speed movements on tracks carrying both freight (including hazardous materials) and passenger trains. At the time of the Red Oak collision, the alerter was programmed to activate about every 2 minutes if no engineer activity was detected. While the train was operating at about 20 mph, it travelled nearly 3,520 feet between each cycle.[76]

The use of restricted speed to allow following trains to enter a block of track occupied by another train is a common and necessary railroad operating practice. Given the limitations of existing alerter technology, it is prudent for railroads to examine the possible role of technology to assist crews in maintaining vigilance as well as to result in intervention when lapses in vigilance occur. Restricted speed is a high-risk railroad operation usually involving following or conflicting movements with the potential for collisions. According to event recorder data, the Red Oak alerter functioned according to specifications and the engineer reset the alerter when it activated. During the critical last 1 minute 53 seconds before impact, no control inputs were made by the crew nor were they required by the alertness device installed on BNSF 9159.

---

[76]The following formula was used to determine this distance: ((20 x 5,280 feet) / 3600 seconds) x (120 seconds) = feet traveled in 2 minutes.

During the last 15 minutes before impact, there were three alerter alarms that were acknowledged by the engineer only after a 5-second strobe was followed by several seconds of audible warning. In previous railroad accident investigations, the NTSB has concluded that a risk of alerters is that they can be reset by reflex action, as if they were "snooze alarms."

The most likely explanation for the striking train engineer's waiting to take action until the audible alarm sounded is that the engineer was asleep, and he was not aware of the alerter alarm until the audible component roused him. If the engineer was asleep, the audible portion of the alerter alarm may have roused him long enough to reset the alarm but not long enough to take continued action to control the train, thus defeating the safety function of the alerter: stopping the train when an engineer becomes incapacitated. This reveals a limitation of alerters: they do not mitigate fatigue but are a last resort to stop a train when an engineer becomes incapacitated and inactive for a prolonged period.

Limitations of Alerters. The FRA Collision Analysis Working Group[77] found that nearly 30 percent of collisions over a 5-year period involved lack of alertness as a probable contributing factor. In those collisions, about 70 percent of the locomotives involved were equipped with alerters. Oman and Liu[78] cite a study by an unidentified major freight railroad indicating that its trains experienced four alerter-induced penalty braking events[79] during the first 6 months of 2006. They extrapolate this number to the U.S. railroad network and estimate that there would have been several dozen such alerter-induced penalty brake applications in a 12-month period. They conclude, "clearly, conventional alerters are not preventing all fatigue and alertness related accidents."

Most important, current alerter technology does not address the underlying cause of fatigue-related inattention: fatigue. A sleeping engineer who is roused by the alerter remains fatigued and is still at higher risk of having an accident. There are a number of initiatives aimed at addressing fatigue before a crew goes on duty. Fatigue training, medical monitoring, and schedule analysis are all proactive approaches that are mandated by the RSIA.

Although addressing fatigue before a fatigued crew is called on duty is a preferred approach, the Red Oak collision and the other fatigue-related accidents investigated by the NTSB suggest that a broader technological approach is needed to help identify fatigued train crews once they go on duty. The optimum strategy is to address fatigue, but alerter devices will remain one element of a risk-mitigation strategy, and other

---

[77] *Collision Analysis Working Group Final Report* (Washington, D.C.: U.S. Department of Transportation, Federal Railroad Administration, 2006).

[78] C.M. Oman and A.M. Liu, Locomotive In-Cab Alerter Technology Assessment, Man Vehicle Laboratory Report #07.30, excerpted from Development of Alternative Locomotive In-Cab Alerter Technology: Final Technical Report (Cambridge, MA: DOT Volpe National Transportation Systems Center, 2006).

[79] An *alerter-induced penalty brake event,* or *brake application*, occurs when an engineer fails to respond to visual and audible warnings for up to 25 seconds, causing the alerter system to stop the train.

technological methods for detecting and addressing fatigued crews on duty need to be explored.

Larger railroads now use technology to monitor engineer train handling performance, in some cases on a near real-time basis. Typically, this is achieved by computer-driven analysis of event recorder data. Exception reports are produced and communicated to managers when certain criteria are met such as emergency braking or fuel-inefficient throttle use. These systems allow timely communication with crews to investigate certain events and to identify the need to provide training and coaching to improve performance where warranted. FRA researchers have previously suggested[80] using event recorder data as an evaluation tool to assess the effectiveness of fatigue management interventions.

The NTSB believes that this same approach may have value for identifying fatigued engineers proactively. Event recorder and alerter data inputs could be used to develop a "fatigue signature" that could result in management intervention. An alerter-induced penalty brake application is one element of such a signature. As geographic databases are created to support PTC, it will be possible, for example, to coordinate locations of grade crossings with whistle use; when a locomotive whistle is not sounded at a crossing, it is often an indicator of crew inattentiveness. In the future, if railroads implement the NTSB's recommendations on inward-facing video cameras,[81] image analysis technology could be used to activate an in-cab alerter device when an engineer appears to have fallen asleep on a moving train, and also to provide an alert to a dispatch center to trigger a timely intervention.

The NTSB concludes that locomotive alerters only detect engineer inactivity and should not be used as a substitute for an effective fatigue mitigation strategy. Therefore, the NTSB recommends that the FRA conduct research on new and existing methods that can identify fatigue and mitigate performance decrements associated with fatigue in on-duty train crews. The NTSB further recommends that the FRA require the implementation of methods that can identify fatigue and mitigate performance decrements associated with fatigue in on-duty train crews that are identified or developed in response to the previous recommendation.

---

[80] M. Coplen and D. Sussman, "Fatigue and alertness in the United states (sic) railroad industry part II: Fatigue research in the Office of Research and Development at the Federal Railroad Administration," *Transportation Research Part F*, January 15, 2001.

[81] *Collision of Metrolink Train 111 With Union Pacific Train LOF65–12, Chatsworth, California, September 12, 2008,* Railroad Accident Report NTSB/RAR-10/01 (Washington, D.C.: National Transportation Safety Board, 2010). <http://www.ntsb.gov>

2.4   Restricted Speed Accidents

2.4.1   Recent Restricted Speed Accidents

Beginning with the Red Oak accident, from April through August 2011, five rear-end collisions of railroad trains occurred in which crewmembers failed to operate their trains at the required restricted speed: (1) Red Oak, Iowa, on April 17, 2011, (2) Low Moor, Virginia, on May 21, 2011, (3) Mineral Springs, North Carolina, on May 24, 2011, (4) DeWitt, New York, on July 6, 2011, and (5) DeKalb, Indiana, on August 19, 2011. Details of these accidents and an additional restricted speed accident that occurred January 6, 2012, are at appendix E.

Information obtained by NTSB investigators indicates that the train crews in the five 2011 accidents failed to operate their trains at the required restricted speeds. Two of the accidents resulted in crewmember fatalities. Four of the accidents occurred on railroad lines over which Amtrak passenger trains operate. Because these accidents occurred on different railroads and under different circumstances, the NTSB is concerned that noncompliance with restricted speed requirements may be an issue affecting a broad segment of the U.S. railroad industry.

During train operations, the signal system or train dispatcher can often provide safe separation between trains moving in either the same direction or the opposite direction. However, there are times when trains must be authorized to occupy the same sections of track. In these cases, safe train operation relies solely on crewmember compliance with the railroad's restricted speed requirements. The NTSB believes all railroads should be informed about the circumstances identified in these accidents. In addition, the NTSB believes all railroads should emphasize adequate training and ensure the compliance of train crews operating at restricted speeds.

Therefore, on January 23, 2012, the NTSB issued safety recommendations to the Association of American Railroads (R-11-8) and to the Brotherhood of Locomotive Engineers and Trainmen and the United Transportation Union (R-11-10):

> Through appropriate and expeditious means, such as issuing and posting advisory bulletins on your website, use the occurrences of five recent rear-end collisions of freight trains—(1) Red Oak, Iowa, on April 17, 2011, (2) Low Moor, Virginia, on May 21, 2011, (3) Mineral Springs, North Carolina, on May 24, 2011, (4) DeWitt, New York, on July 6, 2011, and (5) DeKalb, Indiana, on August 19, 2011—to urge your members to undertake a review of their operations to identify the potential for similar occurrences and to take appropriate mitigating actions. (R-11-8)

On January 12, 2012, the AAR sent an e-mail to the Class 1 railroad officers responsible for rule compliance. In addition, the AAR held a conference call the following day with representatives from each of the Class 1 railroad safety departments and further reviewed the occurrences of the five aforementioned train accidents. As a result, AAR staff reviewed the substantive elements of Safety Recommendation R-11-8 with the AAR Risk Management Working Committee that consists of senior safety and risk managers on all of the Class 1 railroads. Consequently, Safety Recommendation R-11-8 to the AAR is classified "Closed—Acceptable Action."

> Through appropriate and expeditious means, such as issuing and posting advisory bulletins on your website, use the occurrences of five recent rear-end collisions of freight trains—(1) Red Oak, Iowa, on April 17, 2011, (2) Low Moor, Virginia, on May 21, 2011, (3) Mineral Springs, North Carolina, on May 24, 2011, (4) DeWitt, New York, on July 6, 2011, and (5) DeKalb, Indiana, on August 19, 2011—to do the following:
>
> • Emphasize to your members the importance of operating their trains in accordance with restricted speed operating rules.
>
> • Urge your members to work with their employers to identify the potential for similar occurrences and to take appropriate mitigating actions. (R-11-10)

The United Transportation Union published an article in its February 2012 issue of the *UTU News* urging unions, their members, carriers and the FRA to work collaboratively to ensure compliance with speed restrictions by train and engine crews. The article included the following addressing restricted speed:

> Typically, these requirements include being prepared to stop within one-half the range of vision. Complete understanding of, and strict compliance with, restricted speed requirements are absolutely mandatory to prevent catastrophic train collisions.

In addition, the Brotherhood of Locomotive Engineers and Trainmen (BLET) printed a similar editorial in its March 2012 *Locomotive Engineers & Trainmen News* noting, "Emphasize to your members the importance of operating their trains in accordance with restricted speed operating rules." BLET National President Dennis R. Pierce advised the NTSB in a March 2, 2012, letter that he would be making BLET members aware of the rear-end collisions and the need to refocus on operating at restricted speed. He wrote, "I fully agree that operating trains in strict accordance with restricted speed operating rules is a job-saver and a lifesaver." He continued—

> BLET members work in one of the most safety-critical environments in the world, and their increased focus on restricted speed operations in light of these accidents is part of the professional performance of their duties that we intend to stress.

Therefore Safety Recommendation R-11-10 issued to the BLET and the United Transportation Union is classified "Closed—Acceptable Action."

Also on January 23, 2012, the NTSB issued safety recommendations to the Federal Railroad Administration (R-11-6 and -7), to the Association of American Railroads (R-11-9), and to the American Short Line and Regional Railroad Association (R-11-8 and -9). The recommendations are listed in section 4.2, "Previously Issued Recommendations."

2.4.2 Restricted Speed and Positive Train Control

In this accident, had a PTC or Electronic Train Management System[82] (ETMS) been installed on the Creston Subdivision, it would have established the red restricting grade signal as a target and the system would have enforced the upper limit of restricted speed (20 mph on the BNSF). An ETMS onboard locomotive display unit would have shown a "restricted speed fence" (that is, diagonal lines on the display) and would have required restricted speed. Upon reaching 3 mph over the 20-mph restriction (23 mph),[83] a visual alarm would have been displayed and an audible alarm would have sounded. If the engineer did not take action to reduce speed, a full service penalty brake application would have been applied automatically, bringing the train to a stop. If the ETMS had been installed on the Creston Subdivision, as currently designed it would have conveyed a visual and audible warning to the crew when a speed of 23 mph was detected.

In this accident, after passing the red restricting grade signal, had the ETMS been installed, it would have identified the next target as the stop signal at CP McPherson. The ETMS system would have sounded a warning based on the braking profile of the train and initiated automatic braking to stop the train before it reached the CP McPherson stop signal (not the rear of the standing MOW train). The stopped train that stood between the grade signal and the CP McPherson stop signal would not have shown up on the display of the approaching coal train. As the ETMS is currently designed, the rear end of the standing train would not have been a target.

The NTSB, therefore, concludes that had the PTC/ETMS currently in development been installed on the Creston Subdivision, it most likely would not have prevented this accident because it does not identify the rear end of a standing train as a target and because it allows following movements at up to 23 mph. The NTSB emphasized the importance of preventing accidents when trains are operated at restricted speed in its response to the FRA's NPRM, "Positive Train Control Systems," that was published in the *Federal Register* on July 21, 2009. The FRA had mentioned that PTC technology does not protect following trains proceeding at restricted speed into an occupied block (the circumstances in this accident at Red Oak). The NTSB's comments on the proposed rulemaking included the following:[84]

---

[82] ETMS is the system the BNSF is installing to comply with the regulatory requirement for PTC.

[83] Event recorder data indicate that the striking train's speed increased from 22 mph to 23 mph about 5 seconds before impact.

[84] NTSB, Office of the Chairman, To U.S. Department of Transportation, Docket Management Facility, Attention: Docket No. FRA-200800132, Notice No. 1, August 18, 2009.

Train-to-Train Collisions at Restricted Speed

Although the NTSB recognizes that proposed PTC requirements will prevent high-speed collisions, the NTSB also recognizes that railroads may need to move trains at restricted speeds and, as noted in Subpart I, train-to-train collisions at restricted speeds could still occur. Current PTC systems do not track the location of the rear end of each train and do not use the rear location as a target to determine where following trains must stop. The NTSB urges the FRA and the railroads to work on developing technology that will improve the prevention of rear-end collisions at restricted speeds and to incorporate that technology into existing PTS systems as it becomes available.

After receiving the NTSB's concerns, the FRA continued to focus on the absolute speed limit when addressing restricted speed and collision avoidance. The following is an excerpt from the FRA's final rule addressing train-to-train collisions that was published in the *Federal Register* on January 15, 2010:

> To avoid rear end collisions, available PTC technology does not always locate the rear-end of each train, but instead relies on the signal system to indicate the appropriate actions. In this example the PTC system would display "restricted speed" to the locomotive engineer as the action required and would enforce the upper limit of restricted speed (i.e., 15 or 20 miles per hour, depending on the railroad). This means that more serious rear end collisions will be prevented, because the upper limit of restricted speed is enforced.[85]

According to FRA accident data for rear-end train collisions,[86] from 2001 until April 2011 there were 16 collisions attributed to "failure to comply with restricted speed or its equivalent not in connection with a block or interlocking signal." The FRA accident data for the same time period indicate that there were 42 collisions caused by "failure to comply with restricted speed in connection with the restrictive indication of a block or interlocking signal." The collision at Red Oak falls in the second group.

Because the PTC designs that are being deployed are not required to detect the rear of a train as a target, restricted speed collisions can continue to occur. Therefore, the NTSB concludes that the PTC designs that are being deployed and the FRA's final rule on the application of PTC are unlikely to prevent future restricted speed rear-end collisions similar to the 58 rear-end collisions reported to the FRA over the last 10 years or the collision at Red Oak because train speeds at the upper limit of restricted speed are allowed. The NTSB recommends that the FRA require the use of PTC technologies that will detect the rear of trains and prevent rear-end collisions.

---

[85] *Federal Register* vol. 75, no. 10 (January 15, 2010), p. 2610.

[86] Information obtained from website of the Federal Railroad Administration Office of Safety Analysis <http://safetydata.fra.dot.gov/OfficeofSafety/> (accessed February 6, 2012).

2.5   Crash Performance

2.5.1   BNSF Locomotive 9159

Investigators examined the crash performance of BNSF 9159 to understand how the substantial damage occurred. They also evaluated the adequacy of existing locomotive crashworthiness standards in light of the locomotive damage seen in the Red Oak collision.

During the collision sequence, the clip car at the rear end of the struck train immediately folded, derailed, and was displaced north of the track. A powered axle and truck from that car along with other train equipment became lodged in front of the snow plow of BNSF 9159, forming a ramp in front of the locomotive. The next car in the struck train, an 89-foot flatcar outfitted with a specialized loading ramp (scorpion car), rode up and over the trapped equipment in front of BNSF 9159, overrode the locomotive anti-climber, and collided with the modular operating cab. The collision forces lifted and rotated the modular operating cab toward the rear, shearing and separating it from its attachment points. When the modular operating cab separated and rolled rearward, the short hood and collision posts no longer provided the protection intended by the crashworthiness design standards. The cab was then crushed at the rooftop as it rolled into the electrical locker, and the forward-facing window frame was folded forward over the top of the cab. The side walls remained relatively intact below the window line. Diesel fuel from the scorpion car leaked onto the front end of BNSF 9159 and caught fire. Several other flatcars overrode the scorpion car before the striking train came to a stop. The detachment and upending of the cab module and subsequent crushing action exerted forces on the cab occupants that would not have been present had the cab remained fixed to the deck. Because the operating cab rotated into the electrical locker, the rear door was crushed. The NTSB concludes that because the isolated locomotive cab module detached from the deck of the locomotive and was subsequently rotated and crushed, the crew could not have survived.

2.5.2   Locomotive Crashworthiness Standards

BNSF 9159 was constructed to meet the crashworthiness standards in AAR Standard S-580, "Locomotive Crashworthiness Requirements." This standard is incorporated by reference in 49 CFR 229.205 and is applicable to all locomotives built after January 2009. EMD supplied documentation on the structural design and analysis of this model locomotive that confirmed BNSF 9159 was in compliance with these regulatory requirements. However, AAR Standard S-580 does not specifically address modular (isolated) wide-nose locomotive operating cabs like the cab on BNSF 9159.

Current crashworthiness requirements are design standards. Design standards fix requirements under prescribed conditions, which are not necessarily related to the variety of conditions that could occur in a collision. They were based on specific accident scenarios and on locomotive designs in use at the time of their development. In comparison, performance standards attempt to define equipment performance requirements. For example, maintaining survivable space in a control compartment following a collision is a performance standard; prescribing the strength of a collision post in front of the control compartment is a design standard.

Modular cabs are very effective at reducing crew noise and vibration exposure, which can have a safety benefit. There are about 562 isolated cab locomotives operating in North America. Cab integrity is vital to crew safety in a variety of accident scenarios including train-train collisions, train-motor vehicle collisions, and train derailments in which a locomotive overturns. There are no crashworthiness criteria for modular cabs in the existing standards. The NTSB concludes that although the current locomotive crashworthiness standards include a procedure to validate alternative locomotive crashworthiness designs that are not consistent with any FRA-approved locomotive crashworthiness design standard, this requirement was not effective in identifying the modular operating cab as an alternate design.

Consequently, the NTSB recommends that the FRA revise 49 CFR Part 229 to ensure the protection of the occupants of isolated locomotive operating cabs in the event of a collision. Make the revision applicable to all locomotives, including the existing fleet and those newly constructed, rebuilt, refurbished, and overhauled, unless the cab will never be occupied. Finally, to address future locomotive designs, the NTSB recommends that the FRA revise 49 CFR Part 229 to require crashworthiness performance validation for all new locomotive designs under conditions expected in a collision. The NTSB also recommends that the AAR revise its Standard S-580 to provide protection for the occupants of isolated operating cabs in the event of a collision, and make the revision applicable to all locomotives, including those newly constructed, rebuilt, refurbished, and overhauled.

2.6   Emergency Response

The engineer of the struck train activated the 911 emergency response system about 6:57 a.m. The collision occurred in a rural area almost 8 miles from the responding fire department. Logs indicate that responders arrived on scene about 13 minutes after the call. The first on-scene priorities were locating the crew of the striking train and fire suppression. Communication and coordination between responders and the BNSF was described as very good. Therefore, the NTSB concludes that the emergency response to the accident was timely and appropriate.

2.7   Locomotive In-Cab Video and Audio Recorders

The NTSB has long advocated in-cab recording devices in order to better understand crew activities leading up to serious accidents. As a result of its investigation of the collision between a Maryland Rail Commuter train and an Amtrak train near

Silver Spring, Maryland, on February 16, 1996,[87] in which no operating crewmembers survived, the NTSB was unable to determine whether certain crewmember activities leading up to the accident may have contributed to the accident. Consequently, the NTSB recommended that the FRA

> Amend 49 *Code of Federal Regulations* Part 229 to require the recording of train crewmembers' voice communications for exclusive use in accident investigations and with appropriate limitations on the public release of such recordings. (R-97-9)

After its investigation of another railroad accident with no surviving crewmembers that occurred in 1999 in Bryan, Ohio, the NTSB reiterated Safety Recommendation R-97-9 to the FRA. The FRA responded that it

> ... has reluctantly come to the conclusion that this recommendation should not be implemented at the present time. ... [The] FRA appreciates that, as time passes and other uses are found for recording media that may create synergies with other public and private purposes, the Board's recommendation may warrant re-examination.

Based on this response and further meetings, the NTSB classified Safety Recommendation R-97-9 "Closed—Unacceptable Action."

Since the refusal by the FRA to act on the recommendation regarding in-cab recorders, the NTSB has continued to investigate accidents in which such recorders would have provided valuable information to help determine probable cause and develop safety recommendations. As a result of its investigation of the July 10, 2005, collision of two CN freight trains in Anding, Mississippi,[88] the NTSB made the following safety recommendation to the FRA:

> Require the installation of a crash- and fire-protected locomotive cab voice recorder, or a combined voice and video recorder, (for the exclusive use in accident investigations and with appropriate limitations on the public release of such recordings) in all controlling locomotive cabs and cab car operating compartments. The recorder should have a minimum 2-hour continuous recording capability, microphones capable of capturing crewmembers' voices and sounds generated within the cab, and a channel to record all radio conversations to and from crewmembers. (R-07-3)

Most recently, as a result of the investigation into the Chatsworth, California, head-on collision between a Metrolink commuter passenger train and a Union Pacific freight

---

[87] *Collision and Derailment of Maryland Rail Commuter MARC Train 286 and National Railroad Passenger Corporation Amtrak Train 29, near Silver Spring, Maryland, on February 16, 1996*, Railroad Accident Report NTSB/RAR-97/02 (Washington, D.C.: National Transportation Safety Board, 1997). <http://www.ntsb.gov>

[88] NTSB/RAR-07/01. <http://www.ntsb.gov>

train,[89] the NTSB reclassified Safety Recommendation R-07-03 "Closed—Unacceptable Action/Superseded." In that investigation, the NTSB noted that

> In all too many accidents, the individuals directly involved are either limited in their recollection of events or, as in the case of the Chatsworth accident, are not available to be interviewed because of fatal injuries. In a number of accidents the NTSB has investigated, a better knowledge of crewmembers' actions before an accident would have helped reveal the key causal factors and would perhaps have facilitated the development of more effective safety recommendations.

The NTSB reclassified Safety Recommendation R-07-3 "Closed—Unacceptable Action/Superseded" when it issued Safety Recommendation R-10-1 to the FRA:

> Require the installation, in all controlling locomotive cabs and cab car operating compartments, of crash- and fire-protected inward- and outward-facing audio and image recorders capable of providing recordings to verify that train crew actions are in accordance with rules and procedures that are essential to safety as well as train operating conditions. The devices should have a minimum 12-hour continuous recording capability with recordings that are easily accessible for review, with appropriate limitations on public release, for the investigation of accidents or for use by management in carrying out efficiency testing and systemwide performance monitoring programs. (R-10-1)

The NTSB also issued the following Safety Recommendation to the FRA:

> Require that railroads regularly review and use in-cab audio and image recordings (with appropriate limitations on public release), in conjunction with other performance data, to verify that train crew actions are in accordance with rules and procedures that are essential to safety. (R-10-2)

Recommendations R-10-1 and R-10-2 are currently classified as "Open—Acceptable Response."

The rear-end collision near Red Oak again demonstrates the need for in-cab recording devices to better understand (and thereby prevent) serious railroad accidents that claim the lives of crewmembers, passengers, and the public. While video recorders will assist in the investigation of accidents, their value in preventing accidents cannot be overstated. As highlighted in the discussion about the limitations of alerters in section 2.3.3, installation of inward-facing cameras can also assist railroads in monitoring rules compliance and identifying fatigued engineers. Such monitoring can lead to interventions before an accident occurs.

---

[89] NTSB/RAR-10/01. <http://www.ntsb.gov>

Based on medical records, work-rest histories, and event recorder data, investigators determined that the crewmembers of the striking coal train had fallen asleep just before the collision. However, without visual evidence of the crewmembers' actions during the trip, additional information about the crewmembers' performance was not available for investigators. Thus this accident again demonstrates the need for inward-facing video and audio recorders in the cabs of locomotives. The NTSB, therefore, concludes that had an inward-facing video and audio recorder been installed in the cab of the locomotive of the striking train, additional valuable information about the train crew's actions before the collision would have been available.

Based on the important safety and investigative role of inward-facing video and audio monitoring devices, the NTSB reiterates Safety Recommendations R-10-01 and -02.

2.8   Safeguarding Electronic Data for Accident Investigations

The NTSB has long advocated the capture and preservation of onboard locomotive operational data to assist in accident investigations. In the derailment of a Louisville and Nashville freight train in Pensacola, Florida, on November 9, 1977, the NTSB recommended that the FRA

> Promulgate regulations to require locomotives used in trains on main tracks outside of yard limits to be equipped with operating event recorders. (R-78-44)

The FRA responded that "such regulations are not appropriate" and, in a subsequent communication, that "any safety benefit ... is significantly exceeded by the cost of installation and maintenance." The FRA wrote to the NTSB in 1985 that it believed that the intent of the recommendation was being accomplished without regulation and that "Federal involvement is neither justified or necessary." Based on this response, the NTSB classified Safety Recommendation R-78-044 "Closed—Unacceptable Action" on November 29, 1985.

In its investigation of the rear-end collision between two Union Pacific Railroad freight trains in Hermosa, Wyoming, on October 16, 1980, the NTSB made the following safety recommendation to the AAR:

> Encourage member railroads to install or relocate event recorders so as to lessen the likelihood of their becoming damaged in an accident. (R-81-50)

The NTSB classified Safety Recommendation R-81-50 "Closed—Acceptable Action" on December 30, 1982.

After the NTSB's first recommendation on event recorders in 1978, recorder and data storage technology improved and railroads began to install locomotive event recorders in much greater numbers. By the 1990s, most railroads were installing event recorders on their locomotives.

In 1988 Congress passed legislation requiring the FRA to promulgate event recorder regulations, and the requirement for event recorders on all lead locomotives of trains operating above 30 mph became effective in 1995. However, recorder data remained susceptible to damage during accidents, and their value in accident investigation was compromised in many cases.

In its investigation of a head-on collision between two Union Pacific freight trains in Devine, Texas, that occurred on June 22, 1997, the NTSB found that the event recorders on both lead locomotives were destroyed and that critical operational data were lost. The NTSB made the following safety recommendation to the FRA:

> Working with the industry, develop and implement event recorder crashworthiness standards for all new or rebuilt locomotives by January 1, 2000. (R-98-30)

The FRA utilized RSAC to help develop language for an NPRM. Eventually, a regulation requiring crashworthy event recorder memory modules was promulgated and became effective October 1, 2005. In correspondence dated October 26, 2005, the NTSB stated its preference for stricter recorder survivability standards that would meet the European Organization for Civil Aviation Equipment standard.[90] The NTSB noted that the regulatory standards issued by the FRA are less stringent. Nonetheless, the NTSB classified safety recommendation R-98-30 "Closed—Acceptable Action." In a letter dated October 26, 2005, the NTSB further noted that

> ... it will continue to monitor this situation and offer recommendations as a result of its (future) accident investigations to improve the effectiveness of crashworthiness standards and survivability of event recorders.

In the Red Oak accident, data from the forward-facing video recorder on the BNSF 9159 did not survive the collision and subsequent fire because it was not housed in a crashworthy memory module. However, on the same locomotive, event recorder data stored in a certified U.S. Department of Transportation crashworthy memory module did survive and was available to investigators, allowing them to better understand the circumstances of the accident. The NTSB concludes that because the FRA developed standards and regulations for certified U.S. Department of Transportation crashworthy event recorder memory modules in response to the NTSB's prior recommendations, and a crashworthy event recorder was installed on the accident locomotive, information about this accident was available that otherwise would have been destroyed.

Forward-facing video cameras are not required by regulation. The BNSF and many other railroads are voluntarily installing forward-facing video cameras as a good safety practice that allows railroads to obtain factual information and to verify conditions

---

[90] While this is an aviation standard, it is based on fire temperatures more consistent with diesel fuel fires than the 750° C (1400° F) contained in 49 CFR 229.135(b). For example, the locomotive diesel fire following the Anding, Mississippi, collision was estimated to have reached well over 1000° C.

related to incidents involving trespassers, highway-rail grade crossings at grade, and other accidents. These cameras have obvious value for accident investigation and prevention. In the Red Oak accident, this type of video data was not available because the recorder data was not stored in a crashworthy memory module and was lost to collision and fire damage. The NTSB believes that it would be a good safety practice for railroads to ensure that data from these voluntarily installed cameras be safeguarded. The NTSB concludes that because data from voluntarily installed locomotive video cameras are typically not stored in crashworthy memory modules, important operational and safety data are at risk of being lost following an accident. Addressing this risk provides an opportunity for the industry to revisit the best methods to preserve electronic data. As the NTSB has noted, the current regulatory standards allow enclosures to be designed to withstand temperatures as low as 750° C (1400° F), while diesel fires can burn at much higher temperatures. Therefore, the NTSB recommends that the AAR develop a standard that specifies the use of suitable crash-protected memory modules for all new and existing installations of onboard video and audio recorders. The memory modules should meet or exceed the survivability criteria specified in 49 CFR 229.135 Appendix D, Table 2.

3. Conclusions

3.1 Findings

1. The following were not factors in the accident: the condition of the track, railcars, or signal system; the weather; the visibility of signals; the use of cellular telephones by crewmembers; the vision and hearing of the crew; illegal drug or alcohol use, the actions of the train dispatcher and the crew of the maintenance-of-way equipment train; or the mechanical condition of the locomotives of the striking coal train.

2. The striking coal train conductor's and the engineer's irregular work schedules contributed to their being fatigued on the morning of the collision.

3. Based on their medical histories, both crewmembers on the striking coal train were at high risk for sleep disorders and fatigue.

4. Based on the conductor's and the engineer's irregular work schedules, their medical histories, and their lack of action before the collision, both crewmembers on the striking coal train had fallen asleep due to fatigue.

5. Had the two crewmembers on the striking coal train completed the BNSF's fatigue training program, they would have had the opportunity to learn that they were at risk for sleep disorders, particularly obstructive sleep apnea, and the computer-based training program would have displayed a message advising them to consult with a physician.

6. Had the requirements described in Safety Recommendations R-02-24, -25, and -26 been in place, this crew would likely have been identified as at high risk for sleep disorders, which may have led to appropriate medical intervention.

7. Because biomathematical models of fatigue are relatively new to the railroad industry, the use of this technology should be evaluated for its effectiveness within the context of railroads' fatigue management plans through independent scientific peer review.

8. Had the crew of the striking coal train been alert and operated their train in accordance with restricted speed requirements, the collision would have been prevented.

9. Locomotive alerters only detect engineer inactivity and should not be used as a substitute for an effective fatigue mitigation strategy.

10. Had the positive train control/Electronic Train Management System currently in development been installed on the Creston Subdivision, it most likely would not have prevented this accident because it does not identify the rear end of a standing train as a target and because it allows following movements at up to 23 mph.

11. The positive train control designs that are being deployed and the Federal Railroad Administration's final rule on the application of positive train control are unlikely to prevent future restricted speed rear-end collisions similar to the 58 rear-end collisions reported to the Federal Railroad Administration over the last 10 years or the collision at Red Oak because train speeds at the upper limit of restricted speed are allowed.

12. Because the isolated locomotive cab module detached from the deck of the locomotive and was subsequently rotated and crushed, the crew could not have survived.

13. Although the current locomotive crashworthiness standards include a procedure to validate alternative locomotive crashworthiness designs that are not consistent with any Federal Railroad Administration-approved locomotive crashworthiness design standard, this requirement was not effective in identifying the modular operating cab as an alternate design.

14. The emergency response to the accident was timely and appropriate.

15. Had an inward-facing video and audio recorder been installed in the cab of the locomotive of the striking train, additional valuable information about the train crew's actions before the collision would have been available.

16. Because the Federal Railroad Administration developed standards and regulations for certified U.S. Department of Transportation crashworthy event recorder memory modules in response to the National Transportation Safety Board's prior recommendations, and a crashworthy event recorder was installed on the accident locomotive, information about this accident was available that otherwise would have been destroyed.

17. Because data from voluntarily installed locomotive video cameras are typically not stored in crashworthy memory modules, important operational and safety data are at risk of being lost following an accident.

3.2   Probable Cause

The National Transportation Safety Board determines that the probable cause of the accident was the failure of the crew of the striking train to comply with the signal indication requiring them to operate in accordance with restricted speed requirements and stop short of the standing train because they had fallen asleep due to fatigue resulting from their irregular work schedules and their medical conditions. Contributing to the accident was the absence of a positive train control system that identifies the rear of a train and stops a following train if a safe braking profile is exceeded. Contributing to the severity of collision damage to the locomotive cab of the striking coal train was the absence of crashworthiness standards for modular locomotive crew cabs.

4.   Recommendations

As a result of its investigation of this accident, the National Transportation Safety Board makes the following safety recommendations:

4.1   New Recommendations

To the Federal Railroad Administration:

Require railroads to medically screen employees in safety-sensitive positions for sleep apnea and other sleep disorders. (R-12-16)

Establish an ongoing program to monitor, evaluate, report on, and continuously improve fatigue management systems implemented by operating railroads to identify, mitigate, and continuously reduce fatigue-related risks for personnel performing safety-critical tasks, with particular emphasis on biomathematical models of fatigue. (R-12-17)

Conduct research on new and existing methods that can identify fatigue and mitigate performance decrements associated with fatigue in on-duty train crews. (R-12-18)

Require the implementation of methods that can identify fatigue and mitigate performance decrements associated with fatigue in on-duty train crews that are identified or developed in response to Safety Recommendation R-12-18. (R-12-19)

Require the use of positive train control technologies that will detect the rear of trains and prevent rear-end collisions. (R-12-20)

Revise Title 49 *Code of Federal Regulations* Part 229 to ensure the protection of the occupants of isolated locomotive operating cabs in the event of a collision. Make the revision applicable to all locomotives, including the existing fleet and those newly constructed, rebuilt, refurbished, and overhauled, unless the cab will never be occupied. (R-12-21)

Revise Title 49 *Code of Federal Regulations* Part 229 to require crashworthiness performance validation for all new locomotive designs under conditions expected in a collision. (R-12-22)

To the Association of American Railroads:

Revise Association of American Railroads Standard S-580 to provide protection for the occupants of isolated operating cabs in the event of a collision, and make the revision applicable to all locomotives, including those newly constructed, rebuilt, refurbished, and overhauled. (R-12-23)

Develop a standard that specifies the use of suitable crash-protected memory modules for all new and existing installations of onboard video and audio recorders. The memory modules should meet or exceed the survivability criteria specified in Title 49 *Code of Federal Regulations* 229.135 Appendix D, Table 2. (R-12-24)

To the BNSF Railway:

Require all employees and managers who perform or supervise safety-critical tasks to complete fatigue training on an annual basis and document when they have received this training. (R-12-25)

Medically screen employees in safety-sensitive positions for sleep apnea and other sleep disorders. (R-12-26)

4.2   Previously Issued Recommendations

As a result of this accident investigation and four similar accidents, the National Transportation Safety Board issued the following safety recommendations on January 12, 2012:

To the Federal Railroad Administration:

Through appropriate and expeditious means, such as issuing and posting advisory bulletins on your website, advise all railroads of the occurrences of the following five recent rear-end collisions of freight trains in which crewmembers failed to operate their trains at the required restricted speed: (1) Red Oak, Iowa, on April 17, 2011, (2) Low Moor, Virginia, on May 21, 2011, (3) Mineral Springs, North Carolina, on May 24, 2011, (4) DeWitt, New York, on July 6, 2011, and (5) DeKalb, Indiana, on August 19, 2011. (R-11-6)

Through appropriate and expeditious means, inform your inspectors of the details of these accidents to ensure railroads' compliance with restricted speed requirements. (R-11-7)

To the American Short Line and Regional Railroad Association

Through appropriate and expeditious means, such as issuing and posting advisory bulletins on your website, use the occurrences of five recent rear-end collisions of freight trains—(1) Red Oak, Iowa, on April 17, 2011, (2) Low Moor, Virginia, on May 21, 2011, (3) Mineral Springs, North Carolina, on May 24, 2011, (4) DeWitt, New York, on July 6, 2011, and (5) DeKalb, Indiana, on August 19, 2011—to urge your members to undertake a review of their operations to identify the potential for similar occurrences and to take appropriate mitigating actions. (R-11-8)

To the Association of American Railroads and the American Short Line and Regional Railroad Association

Examine the effectiveness of your member railroads' restricted speed and compliance programs. (R-11-9)

4.3 Previously Issued Recommendations Reclassified in this Report

To the Federal Railroad Administration:

Require railroads to ensure that the lead locomotives used to operate trains on tracks not equipped with a positive train control system are equipped with an alerter. (R-07-1)

Safety Recommendation R-07-01, previously classified "Open—Acceptable Action," is reclassified "Closed—Acceptable Action."

To All Class I Railroads:

Ensure that alerters are installed on all your lead locomotives used to operate trains on tracks not equipped with a positive train control system. (R-07-8)

Safety Recommendation R-07-8 issued to the Kansas City Southern Railway Company, previously classified "Open—Await Response," is reclassified "Closed—Acceptable Action."

To the Association of American Railroads:

Through appropriate and expeditious means, such as issuing and posting advisory bulletins on your website, use the occurrences of five recent rear-end collisions of freight trains—(1) Red Oak, Iowa, on April 17, 2011, (2) Low Moor, Virginia, on May 21, 2011, (3) Mineral Springs, North Carolina, on May 24, 2011, (4) DeWitt, New York, on July 6, 2011, and

(5) DeKalb, Indiana, on August 19, 2011—to urge your members to undertake a review of their operations to identify the potential for similar occurrences and to take appropriate mitigating actions. (R-11-8)

Safety Recommendation R-11-8 issued to the Association of American Railroads is classified "Closed—Acceptable Action."

To the Brotherhood of Locomotive Engineers and Trainmen and the United Transportation Union:

Through appropriate and expeditious means, such as issuing and posting advisory bulletins on your website, use the occurrences of five recent rear-end collisions of freight trains—(1) Red Oak, Iowa, on April 17, 2011, (2) Low Moor, Virginia, on May 21, 2011, (3) Mineral Springs, North Carolina, on May 24, 2011, (4) DeWitt, New York, on July 6, 2011, and (5) DeKalb, Indiana, on August 19, 2011—to do the following:

- Emphasize to your members the importance of operating their trains in accordance with restricted speed operating rules.

- Urge your members to work with their employers to identify the potential for similar occurrences and to take appropriate mitigating actions. (R-11-10)

Safety Recommendation R-11-10 is classified "Closed—Acceptable Action."

4.4   Recommendations Reiterated in this Report

To the Federal Railroad Administration:

Develop a standard medical examination form that includes questions regarding sleep problems and require that the form be used, pursuant to 49 CFR Part 240, to determine the medical fitness of locomotive engineers; the form should also be available for use to determine the medical fitness of other employees in safety-sensitive positions. (R-02-24)

Require that any medical condition that could incapacitate, or seriously impair the performance of, an employee in a safety-sensitive position be reported to the railroad in a timely manner. (R-02-25)

Require that, when a railroad becomes aware that an employee in a safety-sensitive position has a potentially incapacitating or performance-impairing medical condition, the railroad prohibit that employee from performing any safety-sensitive duties until the railroad's designated physician determines that the employee can continue to work safely in a safety-sensitive position. (R-02-26)

Require the installation, in all controlling locomotive cabs and cab car operating compartments, of crash- and fire-protected inward- and outward-facing audio and image recorders capable of providing recordings to verify that train crew actions are in accordance with rules and procedures that are essential to safety as well as train operating conditions. The devices should have a minimum 12-hour continuous recording capability with recordings that are easily accessible for review, with appropriate limitations on public release, for the investigation of accidents or for use by management in carrying out efficiency testing and systemwide performance monitoring programs. (R-10-1)

Require that railroads regularly review and use in-cab audio and image recordings (with appropriate limitations on public release), in conjunction with other performance data, to verify that train crew actions are in accordance with rules and procedures that are essential to safety. (R-10-2)

BY THE NATIONAL TRANSPORTATION SAFETY BOARD

DEBORAH A.P. HERSMAN
Chairman

ROBERT L. SUMWALT
Member

CHRISTOPHER A. HART
Vice Chairman

MARK R. ROSEKIND
Member

EARL F. WEENER
Member

Adopted: April 24, 2012

5. Appendixes

5.1   Appendix A: Investigation

The NTSB was notified of the collision between the two BNSF trains near Red Oak, Iowa, on the morning of April 17, 2011, and investigators arrived on scene later that day. The investigator-in-charge and other investigative team members were launched from Washington, D.C.; Los Angeles; and Chicago. There was no Board Member on scene. Investigative groups were formed to study operations, mechanical equipment, track, signals, human performance, locomotive crashworthiness, and data recorders.

Parties to the investigation were the Federal Railroad Administration, the BNSF Railway, the Brotherhood of Locomotive Engineers and Trainmen, Electro Motive Diesel, Inc., and the United Transportation Union.

5.2   Appendix B: BNSF Key to Signal Aspects and Indications

SIGNAL ASPECTS AND INDICATIONS—April 7, 2010

BNSF Railway - SIGNAL ASPECTS AND INDICATIONS

All signals are subject to modification indicated under individual subdivision special instructions.

DISTANT SIGNALS

Aspects shown in Rules 9.1.3 through 9.1.8 may be displayed with a "D" sign on the signal mast to identify the signal as a distant signal. When a "D" sign is displayed, if train is delayed per Rule 9.9 or Rule 9.9.1 between a distant signal and the next signal, proceed prepared to stop short of the next signal. Absolute signals at automatic switches, outside of block system limits, convey main track distant signal information for the other end of the siding.

BLOCK AND INTERLOCKING SIGNALS

Aspects shown in Rules 9.1.3 through 9.1.8 and 9.1.13 may be displayed on signals with or without a number plate on signal mast.

Rule	Aspects of Color Light and Semaphore Signals	Cab Signal Aspects	Name	Indication
9.1.3			CLEAR	Proceed.
9.1.4			APPROACH LIMITED	Proceed prepared to pass next signal not exceeding 60 MPH and be prepared to enter diverging route at prescribed speed.
9.1.5			ADVANCE APPROACH	Proceed prepared to pass next signal not exceeding 50 MPH and be prepared to enter diverging route at prescribed speed.
9.1.6			APPROACH MEDIUM	Proceed prepared to pass next signal not exceeding 40 MPH and be prepared to enter diverging route at prescribed speed.
9.1.7			APPROACH RESTRICTING	Proceed prepared to pass next signal at restricted speed.
9.1.8			APPROACH	Proceed prepared to stop at next signal, trains exceeding 30 MPH immediately reduce to that speed. (Note: *Speed is 40 MPH for Amtrak and Commuter trains.*)
9.1.9			DIVERGING CLEAR	Proceed on diverging route not exceeding prescribed speed through turnout.
9.1.10			DIVERGING APPROACH DIVERGING	Proceed on diverging route not exceeding prescribed speed through turnout prepared to advance on diverging route at the next signal not exceeding prescribed speed through turnout.
9.1.11			DIVERGING APPROACH MEDIUM	Proceed on diverging route not exceeding prescribed speed through turnout prepared to pass next signal not exceeding 35 MPH.
9.1.12			DIVERGING APPROACH	Proceed on diverging route not exceeding prescribed speed through turnout; approach next signal preparing to stop, if exceeding 30 MPH immediately reduce to that speed. (Note: *Speed is 40 MPH for Amtrak and Commuter trains.*)
9.1.13			RESTRICTING	Proceed at restricted speed.
9.1.14			STOP AND PROCEED	Stop, then proceed at restricted speed.
9.1.15			STOP	Stop.

5.3   Appendix C: BNSF 9159 Event Recorder Data from 6:36 a.m. to the 6:55 a.m. Collision

Time	Activity	Speed (mph)	Distance Traveled Since Last Activity
6:36:11 - 6:36:14	Throttle 3 to 2 to 1	34	(Start near CP 4535)
6:38:25	Throttle 1 to 2	27	5,801 feet
6:38:33	Throttle 2 to 3	27	245 feet
6:40:22 – 6:40:42	Locomotive horn pattern sounded by engineer		3,928 feet
6:40:48	Alerter reset by alerter reset button	22	192 feet
6:40:54	Throttle 3 to 4	21	186 feet
No activity for 2 minutes 2 seconds			
6:42:56 - 6:43:02	Alerter alarm begins, 7-second duration: 5 seconds flashing light then 2 seconds light & horn Alerter reset by alerter reset button	16	3,400 feet
6:43:05	Throttle 4 to 5	16	69 feet
6:44:02 - 6:44:05	Throttle 5 to 4 to 5	14	1,283 feet
6:44:22	Throttle 5 to 6	13	338 feet
6:46:10	Throttle 6 to 7	12	1,999 feet
6:47:07	No activity passing grade signal	13	
No activity for 2 minutes 1 seconds			
6:48.11 - 6:48:18	Alerter alarm begins, 8-second duration: 5 seconds flashing light then 3 seconds light & horn Alerter reset by alerter reset button	13	2,224 feet
6:48:55	Throttle 7 to 6	13	689 feet
6:49:00	Manual sand[e] begins	13	93 feet
6:49:42	Throttle 6 to 5	12	752 feet
6:50:48	Throttle 5 to 6	10	1,053 feet

[a] *Manual sand* refers to sand deposited on the rails to provide traction that is manually controlled by the engineer.

Time	Activity	Speed (mph)	Distance Traveled Since Last Activity
6:51:00	Manual sand ends	11	186 feet
No activity for 2 minutes 2 seconds			
6:53:02 - 6:53:09	Alerter alarm begins, 8-second duration: 5 seconds flashing light then 3 seconds light & horn Alerter reset by alerter reset button	17	2,452 feet
6:53:11	Throttle 6 to 5	18	52 feet
6:53:12	Throttle 5 to 4	18	27 feet
No activity for 1 minute 53 seconds			
6:55:05	Collision	23	3,344 feet

5.4   Appendix D: Medications Referenced in Report

Generic Name (Brand Name)	Medication Use
Chlorpheniramine	An antihistamine used to relieve red, itchy, watery eyes; sneezing; itchy nose or throat; and runny nose caused by allergies, hay fever, and the common cold.
Diphenhydramine	An antihistamine used to relieve red, irritated, itchy, watery eyes; sneezing; and runny nose caused by hay fever, allergies, or the common cold. Diphenhydramine is also used to relieve coughing caused by minor throat or airway irritation. Diphenhydramine is also used to prevent and treat motion sickness, and to treat insomnia.
Ezetimibe and simvastatin (Vytorin)	Used to treat high cholesterol in adults and children who are at least 10 years old.
Glyburide and metformin (Glucovance)	Used to treat type 2 diabetes (non-insulin dependent).
Metoprolol (Lopressor)	Used alone or in combination with other medications to treat high blood pressure.
Pioglitazone (Actos)	Used with a diet and exercise program and sometimes with other medications to treat type 2 diabetes.
Pramipexole (Mirapex)	Used to treat the symptoms of Parkinson's disease and is also used to treat restless legs syndrome.
Ranitidine (Zantac)	Used to treat ulcers and gastroesophageal reflux disease (also known as GERD), a condition in which backward flow of acid from the stomach causes heartburn and injury of the food pipe (esophagus). It is also used to treat conditions where the stomach produces too much acid.
Repaglinide (Prandin)	Used to treat type 2 diabetes (a condition in which the body does not use insulin normally and, therefore, cannot control the amount of sugar in the blood).
Ropinirole (Requip)	Used alone or with other medications to treat the symptoms of Parkinson's disease. It is also used to treat restless legs syndrome (RLS or Ekbom Syndrome). RLS is a condition that causes discomfort in the legs and a strong urge to move the legs, especially at night and when sitting or lying down.
Rosuvastatin (Crestor)	Used to lower cholesterol and triglycerides (types of fat) in the blood.
Temazepam (Restoril)	Used on a short-term basis to treat insomnia (difficulty falling asleep or staying asleep).
Valsartan (Diovan)	Used alone or in combination with other medications to treat high blood pressure.
Venlafaxine (Effexor)	Used to treat major depressive disorders, anxiety, and panic disorders.

5.5   Appendix E: Restricted Speed Accidents Since April 2011

May 21, 2011, Low Moor, Virginia: CSX Transportation freight train H75221 collided with stopped CSX Transportation freight train G88219 in Low Moor, Virginia, which is about 170 miles west of Richmond, Virginia. The trains were operating in double-main track territory. Each train had an engineer and a conductor. No crewmember reported an injury as a result of the collision. The locomotive of the striking train derailed, and the last car on the struck train—a grain car—derailed.

Train G88219 had stopped to wait for another train. Train H75221 had two locomotives, one loaded car, and nine empty cars; it was operating eastbound on a restricted signal indication. Train H75221 was descending a grade and had reached a speed of 21 mph, although the restricted speed for the railroad was 15 mph. The conductor said that as train H75221 passed through a curve, he saw the rear car of standing train G88219. The engineer placed the train into emergency braking about 259 feet before the point of collision. At impact, the train was traveling about 13 mph. At the time of the accident, the weather was partly cloudy, and the temperature was 75° F. Damages are estimated at $150,000.

May 24, 2011, Mineral Springs, North Carolina: Northbound CSX Transportation freight train Q19423 struck the rear of northbound CSX Transportation freight train Q61822 in Mineral Springs, North Carolina, about 8 miles south of the CSX Transportation Monroe Yard. The striking train was traveling about 48 mph at the time of the collision, considerably faster than the mandated 15-mph restricted speed. The striking train consisted of 12 intermodal cars, and the struck train consisted of 9 general manifest cars. Each train had two crewmembers—an engineer and a conductor—who were in the lead locomotives. The engineer and the conductor of the striking train were fatally injured. The engineer and the conductor of the struck train sustained minor injuries. The two locomotives of the striking train were engulfed in a subsequent fire. Damages are estimated at $1.6 million.

July 6, 2011, DeWitt, New York: Eastbound CSX train Q 366-05 with 2 locomotives and 58 cars (40 loaded cars and 18 empty cars) struck the rear of CSX train L 156-05 in DeWitt, New York. Both crewmembers on the striking train were transported to a local hospital where they received medical attention and were released. The two locomotives and the lead car of the striking train and the rear three cars of the struck train derailed. In response, local officials evacuated the surrounding area, including several businesses, and closed nearby roads because of the large amount of diesel fuel that was spilled by the lead locomotive of the striking train.

August 19, 2011, DeKalb, Indiana: Westbound Norfolk Southern train 925C347 with 2 locomotives and 21 loaded cars struck the rear of Norfolk Southern train 359B249, which was stopped at milepost CD366 near DeKalb, Indiana. The collision caused nine cars on the rear of the struck train and both locomotives of the striking train to derail. There were no injuries. Both tracks of the main line were blocked, delaying other freight traffic and scheduled Amtrak (National Railroad Passenger Corporation) passenger service.

January 6, 2012, Westville, Indiana: A CSX transportation freight train collided with the rear end of a standing CSX freight train on main track No. 2 at MP BI 224.5. Moments after the injured crew of striking train escaped from the locomotive, another CSX freight train operating on main track No. 1 struck the derailed equipment obstructing their track. As a result of both collisions, the rearmost seven cars of standing train were derailed and 5 locomotives and 18 cars were derailed from the two striking trains. The engineer and the conductor on first striking train were the only crewmembers that were seriously injured. It was clear and 54° F at the time of the accident. The estimated damage was $3.9 million.